W9-AON-942

CONTENTS

INTRODUCTION

Join a gym, start a healthy eating plan, save more money, stop smoking—the list of New Year's resolutions is endless, but how many of them are ever accomplished? According to Scranton Psychology Professor John C. Norcross, Ph.D., less than 10% of New Year's resolutions are achieved. If you are reading this book, there is a good chance that you fall into the large percentage of people who have spent years failing to reach their goals. What is the reason for this? Why is it that the majority of us are incapable of sticking to anything worthwhile? Is failure a natural human tendency? The answer is a simple one—a lack of self-discipline!

This book is about taking full responsibility for where you are now and where you want to be in the next five, ten, fifteen, or twenty years. You will develop the most important skill required to achieve the life you desire—self-discipline.

Kurt Kopmeyer has spent over 50 years researching and studying success principles and has written several books about the secrets of success. One day during a meeting, success coach Brian Tracy asked Kopmeyer to explain which principles, out of all those he has discovered, was most important for success. He responded, *"There are 999 other success principles that I have found in my reading and experience, but without self-discipline, none of them work."*

Self-discipline is like a key—it unlocks the door to personal fulfillment and opens the door to the life you have been dreaming of. With self-discipline, the average person can rise further than intelligence and talent alone will take them, and the ordinary person can become extraordinary. On the other hand, an educated, talented person without self-discipline will rarely rise above mediocrity. My desire is that this book will help you do the following:

- Build habits that will transform your life
- Gain a better understanding of self-discipline and how important it is in your life
- Take control of your habits so that you can take control of your life

You are the only person capable of changing your life—no one can do that for you. The easiest way to change yourself is to change the things you do each day. If you are stuck in a rut, with the same story of failure on repeat year after year, this book will get you out of that rut if you apply the recommended principles.

If you want to achieve something remarkable but you are not sure how to get started on this journey, this book will serve as a manual for how to get there.

If you have attempted to change your bad habits and adopt good ones only to keep falling back into what you know is keeping you stuck, I will teach you how to break the cycle.

If you are unsatisfied with life, you are in a great place because the disgust that you feel for your current circumstances is an indication that you know you are not where you are supposed to be, and you want to change that. Although we don't equate the word "*disgust*" with positive action, being repelled by your life can serve as the motivation you need to turn things around.

For example, seeing a picture of yourself stuffing a piece of pizza into your mouth with your stomach hanging over your trousers can disgust you so much that you throw your hands up in surrender and vow to get in shape. Having your electricity cut off because you failed to pay your bill can disgust you so much that you make the decision once and for all that you are going to become financially stable.

You can have everything you want in life if you are prepared to put in the work, and everything you need to get to your destination is hidden between the pages of this book. If you are ready to stop wasting time on unproductive activities that are leading you in the opposite direction from where you want to go in life, apply the principles you are going to read and expect to experience a major turnaround in your current circumstances.

JOIN OUR PRODUCTIVITY GROUP

In order to maximize the value you receive from this book, I highly encourage you to join our tight-knit community on Facebook. Here you will be able to connect and share productivity strategies in order to continue your growth.

It would be great to connect with you there,

Daniel Walter

To Join, Visit:
www.pristinepublish.com/focusgroup

DOWNLOAD THE AUDIO VERSION OF THIS BOOK FREE

If you love listening to audiobooks on-the-go or would enjoy a narration as you read along, I have great news for you. You can download the audiobook version of *The Power of Discipline* for FREE (Regularly $14.95) just by signing up for a FREE 30-day Audible trial!

Visit: www.pristinepublish.com/audiobooks

YOUR FREE GIFT - MASTER YOUR MORNING

Just thinking about the word "morning" can put a bad taste in people's mouths. A recent study found that one in four Americans hit the snooze button twice before getting out of bed. Forty-nine percent of the same sample stated that waking up late is the main reason they are always late.

In other words, too many of us struggle with productivity, and there are very few people who jump out of bed as soon as their alarm goes off, excited about starting the day.

I want you to take a couple of minutes and think about what your morning usually looks like…

So you don't feel alone in this, I'll start with what mine looked like a little less than three years ago.

- Set my alarm for 6am, hit the snooze button until 7am
- Jump out of bed, shower, get dressed and run out the door
- Get a McDonalds breakfast and eat it on my way to work
- Shout at the drivers on the road because it's their fault I woke up an hour late
- Get to work with two minutes to spare
- Sit at my desk stuffing my face with coffee and snacks all morning to keep my energy levels up

But then I learned about the power of a consistent morning routine and my life changed. I went from thinking I'd never achieve my dreams, to seeing them slowly manifest while I was becoming confident that I could have anything I set my mind to. Let me start by explaining how healthy morning routines are created and why they make us more productive.

If I had to use an alternative word for "routine," I'd use the word "freedom" because that's what it gives us. Think about it like this: what's the first thing you do when you wake up in the morning? Most of you are going to say, "Brush my teeth." That's because it's a habit. Since childhood, we've been trained to brush our teeth as soon as we get out of bed in the morning, so we don't even think about it, we just do it. When you get in your car every morning to go to work, do you sit there thinking about how you're going to drive your vehicle? No, you just put your foot on the accelerator and go because it's a habit. But when you were first learning to drive, your driving instructor had to tell you what to do, and you had to think carefully about it when you were on the road. It may have taken a while, but you got there in the end, didn't you?

Establishing a morning routine works in the same way. Once it becomes a habit, and you're powering through your routine on autopilot, it will give you freedom because you will no longer struggle to succeed.

When we get down to basics, routines are the foundation of life; everything you do is routine, even if you don't think it is. Your bad morning habits of getting up late and having breakfast on the go have become a routine. The way you style your hair is a routine, the location you leave your shoes when you return home is a routine. Can you see my point? Everything is about routine.

The problem is that your current routines aren't doing you any favors. In fact, they're hindering you. Everything you do in the morning has become an enemy of progress, and the longer you continue living this way, the longer your success will be delayed. If you're anything like me, you probably don't know where to start when it comes to establishing a morning routine. I had no idea what I was doing when I started on this journey, but I had some good people in my life who gave me step-by-step instructions, and now I want to give them to you.

In my bonus e-book, *Master Your Morning,* you will learn about the seven habits you need to apply to become that person who jumps out of bed every morning raring to go. Here are three of them:

1. **A Bedtime Routine:** Sleep is one of the most important things you'll do every evening. Sleep is wonderful, we all love sleeping, which is the main reason why so many of you hit the snooze button every morning! You've probably heard that healthy adults need eight hours of sleep a night, right? Arguably, this is true, but what you may not know is that the quality of your sleep is more important than the quantity. Do you wake up feeling drained and tired no matter how many hours of sleep you get? That's because you're not getting good-quality sleep. And the reason is that you've got a terrible night-time routine.

2. **Wake up early:** As you've just read, it's the quality of your sleep that will determine whether you wake up refreshed or not. The first step to dropping the terrible habit of smashing the snooze button every morning is establishing a good bedtime routine so you wake up

feeling refreshed and energized. Waking up early is an essential habit to cultivate if you want to succeed because it gives you a head start on the day.

3. **No Electronics:** Did you know that smartphone addiction is a real thing? I was addicted to my phone, and I had zero awareness of it. Every time it pinged, I would check to see who was messaging me, and I was always on social media. If you're going to get anywhere in life, kicking this habit is essential, and I'll show you how to do it.

Just by pondering these three habits, can you see where you're going wrong? That's just a snippet of what's in store for you in *Master Your Morning*. You will have access to an abundance of helpful information that will kickstart your journey toward success and get you one step closer to living your dream life.

If you've got to that point where you're sick and tired of being sick and tired, this book is for you. It will equip you with everything you need to become more productive and start taking control of your life instead of letting life control you!

Get *Master Your Morning* for Free by Visiting

www.pristinepublish.com/morningbonus

CHAPTER 1:

SELF-DISCIPLINE - THE BIOLOGICAL ARGUMENT

The assumption is that some people are endowed with self-discipline and others are not, but this is not the case. There is a science to self-discipline, and if you want more of it in your life, it will help you get a better understanding of its biological basis. In this chapter, you will learn about the biology of self-discipline and how you can target certain areas of the brain to improve it.

The human brain contains an estimated 100 billion neurons, the minuscule cells responsible for our behaviors and thoughts. Neuroscientists Todd Hare and Colin Camerer conducted a study in 2009 in which they used functional magnetic resonance imaging machines (fMRIs) to record the brain activity that takes place when people are engaging in tasks that require them to use self-control and discipline. The participants were given a choice between accepting a small financial reward at the immediate conclusion of the study or a larger financial reward at a later date. The researchers induced the classic battle between delayed gratification and willpower. They discovered that there was a high level of activity in two areas of the brain called the ventral medial prefrontal cortex and the dorsolateral prefrontal cortex when participants were making decisions based on the choices made immediately or in the future. The activity in these regions of the brain was higher when choices were made that would benefit them in the long term.

The study concluded that some people find self-discipline easier than others based on the activity and the structure of their prefrontal cortex. The findings of this research are very significant because they highlight the fact that we cannot decide to become more self-controlled and expect to be successful if we haven't developed the skill previously. When you make healthy choices, self-discipline is strengthened; on the other hand, making unhealthy choices diminishes self-discipline. If you find it difficult to say no to sweet treats, you can't stick to an exercise routine, or you can't stop scrolling through YouTube to do something more productive, don't worry, there is still hope for you because you can improve your self-discipline.

DELAYED GRATIFICATION

In 2011, the participants of the Stanford Marshmallow experiment were re-evaluated. The Stanford Marshmallow Experiment took place in 1972, and it was discovered that the participants who found it easier to delay gratification experienced increased activity in the prefrontal cortices. There were also differences in the ventral striatum (the area of the brain linked to addictions) when they were using self-control to make a decision between healthy and unhealthy options. It was also found that the participants who were able to delay gratification were more successful in all areas of life in comparison to the participants in the immediate gratification group. The study revealed that a decision as simple as choosing whether to eat a marshmallow immediately or later determined the way they made decisions in adulthood.

The evidence from studies on self-discipline does not point to genetic predisposition as to why some people have higher levels than others. However, we can conclude that self-discipline is a skill you can master if you are willing to put the work in. Weightlifting strengthens the body, and if you target the areas in the brain mentioned in the studies, they will increase in strength.

If you are reading this book, there is a chance you are struggling with self-discipline. I would like to encourage you not to feel saddened by your current circumstances. There is no denying that any skill is easier to master during childhood; however, that does not rule out the possibility of improving your self-discipline now. When exercised consistently, willpower and self-discipline will improve, and you will experience lasting results. All skills operate under the same principle—the more you practice, the better at it you will become.

FOCUS AND EXECUTIVE FUNCTIONS

Your level of focus will affect the extent of your self-discipline. Neuroscientists believe that your ability to focus is determined by your "executive functions," including working memory, cognitive flexibility, adaptability, and impulse control. Discipline requires you to set goals, filter distractions, control unhelpful inhibitions, prioritize activities, and pursue the goals that you have set. Research states that these functions operate in a number of brain regions, including the anterior cingulate cortex, the orbitofrontal cortex, and the dorsolateral prefrontal cortex. You can improve these brain functions by targeting them. Self-discipline and focus work simultaneously. You can't master one without the other because discipline is the ability to focus on one course of action until that goal has been accomplished.

WILLPOWER FATIGUE

In the same way as the body gets tired after it has been put through a strenuous workout, willpower and self-discipline also lose strength when they have been put to work and worn down. Since there is a biological basis to these skills, the brain of a person who said "no" to a slice of cake 10 times is different from the brain of the person who eats the slice of cake each time it is offered to them. This means that even if an individual is extremely self-disciplined with a lot of willpower, it will eventually run out if they are continuously faced with temptation. In the same way it is impossible for a person to lift weights for 24 hours without a break, it is also impossible for a person to exercise their willpower for 24 hours without taking the time out to replenish it.

In 1996, psychologist Will Baumeister conducted a study in which he evaluated a phenomenon known as willpower depletion. The study involved leaving 67 participants in a room with freshly baked sweet treats and bitter radishes. One group was allowed to eat the sweet treats, while the other group was told to eat the bitter radishes. They were then taken to another room where they were asked to solve a puzzle to evaluate their persistence. The radish eaters did not have the strength of mind to resolve the puzzle and gave up before the group who had eaten the sweet treats. The radish eaters' inability to focus on the task resulted from the fact that their willpower had already been depleted in the previous task, and now they wanted to take the path of least resistance.

WILLPOWER PROTECTION

The main priority for the brain is survival. Today we have enough knowledge to know that temporary low sugar and low energy levels are not life-threatening. However, because of the biology of the brain, it does not know this, and as soon as it receives a warning message that something in the body is out of alignment, it protects you by going into survival mode. When the brain is operating in survival mode, it begins to crave instant gratification, which leads to binge eating and other negative behaviors linked to a lack of self-discipline. Therefore, the best way to build self-discipline is to remove yourself from temptation. For example, if you are struggling with your diet, replace your cupboard of unhealthy foods with healthy choices and meals. When you go grocery shopping, stay away from the aisles selling sweet treats and immediately make your way to the aisles stocking healthy foods. By using these strategies, your willpower is only tested during the time you spend in the store, as opposed to trying to resist the temptation to eat your stash of cookies in the cupboard every evening over and over again.

Another way to protect your willpower is to go shopping after dinner. You won't be hungry because you've just consumed a filling healthy meal, which means you are less likely to buy a bag of chips to hold you over until dinner. What you are doing here is creating conditions in which your vulnerability is not used against you, and you are not forced to use self-discipline. Even if you don't struggle with healthy eating, you can use the same strategies for any areas of your life where you lack self-discipline.

Stress is another biological factor that contributes to willpower. When we are under pressure, the body protects itself by going into 'fight or flight' mode. In this state, we are more likely to act on impulse and do things without thinking. The prefrontal cortex malfunctions when we experience stress, and the brain is only capable of functioning on short-term outcomes. When the prefrontal cortex is not operating at its full potential, we are more likely to make bad decisions.

The principle of discipline is simple—as a mentally stable adult, you know the difference between right and wrong. You understand that if you choose to watch Netflix instead of working on your goals, you will never achieve them. Discipline is about doing what you know you've got to do even when you don't feel like it. But for your efforts to make a difference, you must be consistent. Slacking off every other day isn't going to get you to your destination any more quickly. Consistency builds momentum and that's how dreams become a reality. When you are aware of what discipline demands, you are more likely to choose to do the right thing.

Remember, there is a biological process to discipline, and similarly to any other habit, the brain is programmed to accept it as the norm the more you practice it. There are several benefits associated with self-discipline that I will discuss in the next chapter.

CHAPTER 2:

THE BENEFITS OF SELF-DISCIPLINE

Self-discipline is required for every area of life, but most people don't realize it because society has taught us to float through life on autopilot. I believe that one of the most underrated reasons for the breakdown of the family is a lack of self-discipline. If your partner is cheating, or exhibiting other issues, one of the underlying causes is their inability to control their urges towards the opposite sex. If your partner is running up credit card bills or has other financial issues, one of the reasons is their inability to control their spending habits. In other words, your level of self-discipline will control your level of success in your place of employment, relationships, finances, academics, etc. There are many benefits associated with self-discipline.

RAISES YOUR SELF CONFIDENCE

A lack of self-discipline contributes to low self-esteem. There are many reasons people suffer from low self-esteem, and one of them is that they are not where they need to be in life. People set goals all the time, especially at the beginning of the year, but by the second or third month, they have lapsed back into old habits and their goals are forgotten. Most people fail in life because they don't do what is required for success. The person who wants to lose weight sits on the couch eating burgers, flipping through magazines, and wishing they could wear a bathing suit on vacation. You will never get into a bathing suit sitting in front of the TV dreaming. You want to start earning more money but can't find the motivation to start learning about being self-employed. Inactivity leads to one place—failure. And when five and ten years pass us by in the blink of an eye and we are still stuck in a place we know we don't want to be, a feeling of worthlessness sets in.

A self-disciplined person is confident because, regardless of where they are at that moment, they know that they are the best version of themselves. They are eating properly, exercising, and working towards their goals. They feel good about life because they are in the driver's seat, and they know exactly where they are going.

BUILD BETTER RELATIONSHIPS

One of the main reasons friendships break down is because people do not do what they say they are going to do. You confide in someone only to find out that your entire office now knows your business or a friend borrows money and never pays it back. Friendships and relationships are about trust. A person with self-discipline is always going to live by their word; if you ask them to keep a secret, they will. They are often the same person in private as they are in public because they value integrity. These are rare traits and the world values them; therefore, a disciplined person is more likely to have a strong network of personal relationships because they are trustworthy.

YOU WILL STOP BEING OFFENDED

When people are easily offended, it's because they are not self-assured; they don't know who they are or what they stand for, and so they view criticism (even when it is constructive) as an attack on their character and become deeply offended. Self-disciplined people don't have this problem. They are confident, calm, and self-assured, and so it's easy for them to take insults and criticisms on the chin. Self-disciplined people can handle constructive criticism—in fact, they value it because it pushes them to become better.

AVOID RISKY BEHAVIORS

Behavioral theories attempting to explain risky and unhealthy behaviors often evaluate the role of self-control. For example, Hirschi's and Gottredson's self-control theory states that criminal behavior is due to an individual's inability to control their desire to engage in such behavior. Obviously, there is more to committing crime than a lack of control, but the point is that when morals and the fear of incarceration are removed from the equation, most people would rob a bank instead of work for a living. But the average person has enough self-control not to take that path.

In a 2012 study conducted by Ford and Blumenstein, it was found that American college students with a high level of self-control were less likely to abuse prescription medication, binge drink, or use cannabis.

Research also suggests that there is a relationship between a lack of self-control and impulsive sexual behavior. The participants in the Ford and Blumenstein study were more likely to engage in deviant sexual activity with people who were not their primary partners, all of which increase the risk of sexually transmitted disease and unplanned pregnancy.

There is more to self-discipline than goal attainment, and exercising a consistent high level of self-control will benefit you in many areas of life. You purchased this book because you want to know how to increase your level of self-discipline; however, before we get to that, it's important for you to understand why you find it so difficult to make positive changes in your life.

CHAPTER 3:

THE STATUS QUO BIAS - WHY WE RESIST CHANGE

I applaud you for wanting to improve your self-discipline; but it's important to understand that this is not an easy task. Along your journey you are going to experience mental blockages that prevent you from moving forward. Some people give up altogether when they encounter this type of obstacle and assume that this path is only for the select few. However, when you are familiar with the psychology of self-discipline, you will find it easier to overcome such challenges, which is the main focus of this chapter.

You may know exactly what you want to achieve. You have conquered your fear of failure and your self-discipline levels are improving. Unfortunately, sometimes it feels as if there is an invisible force holding you back. This is extremely frustrating and very common, so please don't feel like you are the only one experiencing it. In this chapter, you will learn about a psychological phenomenon called the "status quo bias" and how it can attack the most self-disciplined and determined individuals. The good news is that once you understand how it works, you can fight against it and continue pushing toward your goals.

The Sunk Cost Fallacy

In psychology, one of the most well-known self-defeating behaviors is the "sunk cost fallacy." It explains why people remain stuck in their circumstances even though they would rather be elsewhere. Some examples are staying in an unfulfilling relationship or keeping a safe but boring job even though you have the opportunity to get better employment. The status quo bias describes the human disposition to cling to what we are familiar with instead of reaching for the unknown. Similar to the Pareto Principle (discussed in chapter 17), the concept has its roots in economics and was founded by economists Richard Zeckhauser and William Samuelson. In 1988, they published a series of studies in the *Journal of Risk and Uncertainty*. The articles highlighted the fact that even though economics attempts to predict the choice a person will take when faced with more than one alternative, in the real world, most people choose to do nothing and carry on as normal. A more general term for this tendency is 'inertia.'

Loss Aversion Theory

Why is it that we choose to stick with the same jobs, people, and ambitions? A number of reasons have been put forward to explain this behavior. One reason is based on the "loss aversion theory," which stipulates that in general, people don't like losing things, and this is true even if the thing they lose wasn't of high value. Before moving onto something that is perceived as better, we want evidence to prove that it is going to enhance our lives before detaching ourselves from what is not serving us. Although making a change often leads to a more positive outcome, on a subconscious level, we assume that change will do us more harm than good.

Even positive change, such as moving to a nicer home or getting married, requires a lot of thought. There is always a cost associated with change, and most of the time, we don't want to pay the price.

THE FEAR OF REGRET

Another reason for the status quo bias is the fear of regret—no one wants to make a change and then regret it. Typically, this is because they feel that friends, family members, or loved ones will judge them for their mistakes. As a result of this fear, they default to sticking to what they are comfortable with. The fear of failure is why people don't like change, but the reality is that failure is not final—it's not the end of the world if you don't get it right. All successful people fail at some point in their lives, but they use their mistakes to make better decisions in the future.

THE MERE EXPOSURE EFFECT

Another powerful mind trick that keeps us bound to the same old behaviors, beliefs, and routines is "the mere exposure effect." Decades of research have found that the more we experience a particular phenomenon, the more we are likely to accept and like it. For example, a study conducted in 1968 found that the more participants were exposed to symbols and words, the chances of developing a positive affiliation with them increased. You may have experienced this in your personal life, where the more you interact with an individual, the more you find yourself liking them. There are definitely exceptions to this rule because in some cases the more you are exposed to something the more you notice things that you don't like. However, in general, the longer we are exposed to a situation, the more we develop an assumption that it may not be exactly what we want, but it will do.

The mere exposure effect has its advantages and disadvantages. The good news is that if you are working toward improving your self-discipline and developing better habits, when self-control becomes the norm to you, there is less chance of you reverting back to your old ways. The more time you spend operating with a positive mindset, the more you will become comfortable with it. The disadvantages are that the natural human tendency to hold on to bad habits will make it difficult to develop good habits. You might have a desire to get up on Saturday morning and start working on your goals, but because you've spent the majority of your life sleeping in on Saturdays, you will have a hard time dismantling your status quo bias. The trick is to keep reminding yourself that the more you get up early, the easier it will become.

Now that you have a better understanding of the status quo bias, think back to times in your life when you have attempted, or had the opportunity, to change something about your life but you failed to persevere because of your status quo bias. Maybe you found yourself saying things like, "*Well, I've always done things like this so there's no point in changing it now.*" Or, "*I can't see that there's any major problem here, so it doesn't make sense to change anything.*"

Remember that the status quo bias is guaranteed to do one thing—and that is to keep you safe. It will also ensure that your hopes and dreams are never fulfilled, and in the long run, you will probably regret not taking action. People shouldn't be afraid of failure; they should be scared of regret. The feeling of looking back on your life and wondering "What if……" will torment you worse than the feeling of having tried and failed. Fortunately, having some self-awareness about this will help you make better decisions in the future.

THOUGHT EVALUATION EXERCISE

Make a promise to yourself that starting today, you are going to put your rational decision-making abilities to good use and build the life you want. Whenever you are faced with the choice of remaining in your current circumstances or doing something to change them, challenge yourself to go through an exercise that will encourage you to evaluate your thoughts in a logical manner:

- Get a piece of paper and draw one line down the middle and one across so there are four quarters.
- In each quarter write the following: Status quo advantages; status quo disadvantages; advantages to the alternative; and disadvantages to the alternative.
- Spend at least ten minutes working on the lists.
- Go to bed and return to the list the following day.
- Ask someone you trust to help you if you want a second opinion or you are afraid you might overlook something.
- Remember to remove your feelings from the decision-making process.

Now that you can visualize your thought process, make the decision to do something that's going to get you out of your comfort zone. Get into the habit of questioning your decisions so that you are actively paying attention to your habits and altering them to ensure that you reach your end goal.

The next step in improving your self-discipline is being realistic about your abilities. I will discuss this in the next chapter.

CHAPTER 4:

A REALITY CHECK - THE DUNNING - KRUGER EFFECT

Confidence is a great thing; it's important that you know what you are good at and you don't doubt yourself in that area. However, it is equally as important that you are familiar with your weaknesses. In this chapter, you will learn about the dangers associated with the inability to assess your competencies and how you can protect yourself against it.

We all know someone who is out of touch with reality when it comes to assessing their skills. For example, the co-worker who thinks they've got such a good sense of humor, but their jokes are never funny! You might not have this problem, but it's helpful to understand it as you never know what the future holds.

THE DUNNING-KRUGER EFFECT

The Dunning-Kruger Effect occurs when an individual is not only incompetent in a certain area but fails to realize how bad they are at it. The person suffering from this issue has what is referred to as a "double burden," which means they are continuously making mistakes in the same area. It is difficult for people to correct them because they are completely ignorant of their deficiencies. Instead of trying to improve their skills, they will continue moving in that direction because they truly believe in their abilities and will argue that their failure is because of bad luck.

Psychologists David Dunning and Justin Kruger from Cornell University discovered that this phenomenon becomes apparent when people are tested on their humor, logic, and grammatical knowledge. They found that those who scored the lowest in these categories were less likely to believe they had a problem in these areas because they suffer from non-existent or weak metacomprehension, metamemory, and metacognition. They are incapable of evaluating their own thinking processes or providing constructive criticism of their own abilities. Prior to this study, it had already been established that people have the tendency to think of themselves more highly than their abilities warrant in areas such as written expression and leadership skills. The Dunning-Kruger Effect simply emphasizes this common human tendency. However, it can also have a negative impact in certain environments. One example is senior managers who are clearly incompetent yet still manage to get promoted. If you haven't already noticed, incompetent people are typically oblivious to their incompetence. They literally walk around with their head in the clouds believing they are the cleverest people in the world. On the other hand, those with a high skill set are usually very modest about their capabilities.

THE RELATIONSHIP BETWEEN SELF-DISCIPLINE AND THE DUNNING-KRUGER EFFECT

So, what is the relationship between self-discipline and the Dunning-Kruger Effect? Self-discipline and self-control are skills, which means it's possible to overestimate your ability in these areas. If you ever get to the point where you believe you have mastered the art of being highly productive at all times and have the ability to resist temptation, be careful! It could be true—maybe you have come a long way—but there could be the possibility that you've still got a lot more work to do. Research suggests that the more familiar you become with something, whether it's a skill or a subject, the likelihood that you will claim you are are an expert diminishes. In other words, the deeper you get into something, the more you realize how much more there is to learn about it.

THE SOLUTION

What is the solution to this paradox? This issue is resolved by striking a balance between confidence that you are proficient in certain areas and being willing to accept constructive criticism. By taking this approach, you will ensure that you never become complacent and live in ignorance about your deficiencies. An example of a chance to use this enlightenment is as follows. Assuming that you are a really good driver, and you register to take an advanced driving course to get a reduction on your insurance premiums, you book some lessons to prepare for the test, but during practice you are told that your driving skills are below average and you are in no way ready to take the test. At this point, you can either accept the constructive criticism and keep practicing, or you can accuse the instructor of being ignorant because *"You're such a good driver."*

A reality check can be disappointing, especially when we think we've made good progress; however, it can also shine a light on the areas we need to improve. Combined with objective feedback, the best way to protect yourself against the Dunning-Kruger Effect is to keep developing yourself. Never assume that you've made it and always aim to be better today than you were yesterday. Additionally, you can take courses or download an app designed to help you improve your skills and knowledge in a certain area. Apps do things like provide you with objective feedback and keep a log of your test scores so you can keep track of how much you have or have not improved.

Another protection strategy against the Dunning-Kruger Effect is to associate with people who are further ahead than you are in the specialty in which you wish to gain competence. Please note, this is not about comparing yourself to others, but about putting yourself in a position where you are exposed to continuous learning. Also, keeping track of where you are now and the goal you want to achieve will keep you grounded.

Be warned! Now that you have knowledge about the Dunning-Kruger Effect, you will start noticing it more, and you may find you are tempted to point the finger at people, especially if it's someone you are not too fond of. When you do experience this, resist the urge to say something. Not only is it not nice, but how would you feel if the shoe was on the other foot?

Finally, remind yourself that there is no such thing as perfection. All humans have flaws, which is a good thing because it means there is always room for improvement.

Now you are ready to gain some insight into the daily habits required to improve self-discipline.

CHAPTER 5:

DAILY HABITS TO IMPROVE SELF-DISCIPLINE

Habits are routine behaviors performed without putting any conscious thought into them. Most of us don't need any motivation to brush our teeth in the morning. All parents train their children from an early age to brush their teeth when they wake up and before going to bed at night. In adulthood, no matter how tired you are, you will brush your teeth in the morning and at night; the habit of brushing your teeth has been hardwired into your brain. The aim of this book is for the actions required to achieve your dreams to become as natural as brushing your teeth, or as natural as some of the bad habits you currently have. Some of you reading this have a bad habit of coming home from work and sitting in front of the TV until it's time to go to bed. My father had this habit, and as children, we knew his every move from the moment he walked through the door. He would greet us in the living room, go upstairs, take off his tie, use the bathroom, come downstairs, dish out a plate of food, and then sit in front of the TV. He did this Monday through Friday without fail.

YOUR HABITS ARE A REFLECTION OF YOUR CHARACTER

Your habits become a part of your character, and some people take pride in the fact that they are known for something. If your friends always tell you to meet them an hour earlier than everyone else, it's because they know you are going to be late, which means you've got a bad habit of being late. Lateness is a part of your life; it's a negative cycle that starts with you going to bed late, waking up late, and then being late for everything else. Or you might binge eat when you are under pressure instead of confronting the issue. According to psychologists, habits of this nature are formed because of the connection between the stimulus and a response. Actions are triggered by thoughts, and as this pattern is repeated, it's only a matter of time before the action becomes a habit and starts to have an impact on your life. Unless a conscious decision to change the behavior is made, it will become permanent.

DAILY HABITS TO IMPROVE SELF-DISCIPLINE

There is only one difference between successful and unsuccessful people, and that is the habits they follow each day. Incredibly successful people perform the same habits every day. They have a set routine and they stick to it. Everything they do improves them mentally, physically, and spiritually. Here are some habits you can start incorporating into your life to improve your level of self-discipline:

YOUR MORNING ROUTINE

Your morning routine will set the pace for the rest of your day. Do you keep hitting the snooze button so that by the time you get out of bed it's too late to go for the morning jog you've had on your to-do list for the last couple of months? Since you woke up late, you have no time to make breakfast and instead stop off at the McDonald's drive-through on your way to work. Because of the way your day has started, you are in the wrong frame of mind to do anything productive and your thought process will be something along the lines of, *"Since I've already had McDonald's for breakfast, I might as well get Taco Bell for lunch. There's no point in me going to the gym after work because I've already eaten all this unhealthy food. I might as well go home, watch Netflix, and start again tomorrow."*

Bad habits are developed by failing to do the most important things in the morning. When you get out of bed as soon as the alarm goes off, exercise, and eat something healthy for breakfast, you will feel so energetic and positive that you will want to keep making healthy decisions throughout the day. You don't need to have an elaborate morning routine, but there are some main habits that all successful people incorporate into their lives before their workday begins, for example:

- Barack Obama starts his day at 7 a.m. He spends 45 minutes exercising, has breakfast, and then makes his way to work.
- Bill Gates is up at 4 a.m. He watches an educational DVD while he's working out on the treadmill, he has breakfast, and then starts working.
- Oprah Winfrey is up at 6:00 a.m. She takes her dogs for a walk, reads positive affirmations, and then meditates before starting her day.

There is a clear pattern here—successful people have a fixed morning routine that enhances their life.

THE FINAL HOUR OF THE DAY

You have just read that what you do first thing in the morning sets the tone for your day. Your evening routine before going to bed at night is just as important as your morning routine.

Sleep is essential for renewing the body, resting the mind, and recharging our batteries so we can be productive the next day. A bedtime routine that allows you to unwind and prepare for the day to come is crucial. Simple things such as turning off all digital equipment and/or reading is a powerful way to decompress, relax, and prepare you for a good night's rest. It is also important to get a minimum of seven hours of sleep each night. Not only does a lack of sleep hinder your productivity, in the long run, it will damage your health.

The following are several other habits that successful people incorporate into their lives each day.

PRACTICE GRATITUDE

In 2016, DeSteno and Dickens conducted a study and found that the more self-control a person had, the more grateful they were. The study involved participants completing a task on the computer. The computer intentionally broke down and another participant helped to resolve the issue. The researchers also evaluated happiness, self-control, and patience in the daily life of the participants over a few weeks. Finally, self-control was measured by offering them a small sum of money as soon as the task was completed or a larger sum of money later on. The study found that there was a strong relationship between gratitude and self-control. The most grateful participants were prepared to wait longer for the financial reward than the less grateful participants. Here are a few things you can do to become more grateful:

- **Say Thank You:** We often take the things people do for granted. We can eliminate this oversight by saying "thank you" for the small things instead of waiting for someone to do something mind-blowing. If you are in a relationship, thank them for being a beautiful person; if you've got kids, thank them for being so loving; thank your friends for being such amazing friends. The aim here is to say thank you and really mean it and feel a sense of appreciation.

- **Make Time for Gratitude:** Another bad habit is constant complaining. It's easy to complain—we live in a world with terrible things going on. It's not difficult to turn on the TV, flip through the newspaper, or listen to the news and assume that there is no hope. However, it's important not to focus on the negative because there are just as many positive things taking place in the world. Every morning, or before you go to bed at night, write down five things you are grateful for. Think about them and feel a deep sense of appreciation and gratitude for what you have written down.

SET DAILY GOALS

You can achieve your long-term goals by breaking them down and setting daily goals for yourself. A big dream can seem daunting, especially when you look at your current situation and realize how far away from it you are now. However, when you break the goal down into small actionable steps, it becomes a lot easier to achieve. When you set daily goals, you build momentum, and that inspires you to keep pushing toward your ultimate goal because you know you are getting closer to it every day.

Setting daily goals isn't about giving yourself random things to do every day, it's about achieving your long-term goal. So for example, let's say you want to lose 60 pounds. You look in the mirror every day saying that you need to lose weight, but because you know you need to lose so much, you keep putting it off until tomorrow. Before you know it, you've gained another 10 pounds! The thought of losing 60 pounds is scary, but if you say you want to lose 60 pounds in 12 months, which works out to 5 pounds a month and just over 1 pound a week, now your goal isn't so intimidating.

You can now start working daily toward that goal. It could involve eating a large portion of vegetables and cutting down on carbs, doing ten minutes of cardio per day, and/or drinking more water. Whatever it is, just make sure you are doing it daily because consistency is the key to your success.

A Good Night's Sleep

Sleep is essential to your productivity. If you are tired and sluggish and feel like you haven't had enough sleep, it will be impossible to get anything done. Here are some tips for getting a great night's sleep every night:

- **Daytime** Naps: If you take naps during the day, limit them to 30 minutes at a time. A short nap can help you feel rested, alert, and improve mood and performance. If you sleep for any longer than 30 minutes during the day, though, you will find it difficult to fall asleep at night.

- **Avoid Stimulants:** Caffeine and nicotine in the evening will stimulate the brain to stay awake, and even when you do manage to fall asleep, you won't experience the deep sleep required to feel rested in the morning.

- **Watch What You Eat:** Rich, heavy, fatty foods and carbonated drinks cause indigestion, which can cause painful heartburn in the middle of the night and interrupt your sleep.

- **A Bedtime Routine:** Prepare the body for sleep by establishing a relaxing bedtime routine. Take a warm bath, read a book, or do some light stretches. You should also avoid emotionally-charged conversations during this time because it could disrupt your sleep.

- **The Right Environment:** A comfortable mattress and pillows will help you sleep a lot better. Make sure that there are no lights from a television, cell phone, or laptops; eyeshades and blackout curtains will block out the light even further.

Stay Organized

Organization and self-discipline go hand in hand. It is impossible to find a self-disciplined person who isn't organized. One of the characteristics of a self-disciplined person is that they want to make life easier for themselves, and one way of doing this is to be organized. Here are some benefits of staying organized:

- **Improves Productivity:** Disorganization creates chaos—you are constantly looking for things, everything is in a mess, and life is a constant battle. Staying organized means you will have more time to spend on the things that matter because you are not wasting all your time looking for things.

- **Less Stress:** How do you feel when you can't find your car keys or those important documents you need for work? Stressed, right? When everything is housed in its rightful place, files and folders are neatly organized, you will eliminate the stress of searching for your items.

- **More Energy and Enthusiasm:** When you are forced to dig through piles of paperwork, clothes, or other objects to find what you need, it drains your energy. When you have no energy, you lack enthusiasm and it becomes impossible to do the things that you know you should be doing.

- **A Positive Image:** Not only will you feel better about yourself because you now have some order to your life, but other people will notice it. If you once had a reputation for being the "disorganized one," friends, family members, and colleagues will start praising you for the orderly and systematic person that you truly are.

PERFORM THESE TWO HABITS BEFORE 8 AM

As you have read, successful people incorporate a number of habits into their daily routine, but during my research, I have found there are two thing successful people do before 8:00 a.m.:

1. **They Pray/Meditate:** Prayer and meditation is a top priority in every religion; even atheists who do not believe in a higher power spend time reflecting and meditating. People from all backgrounds are taking advantage of the benefits of mindfulness and use them as a way to enhance their personal lives.

Research has found that meditation is an effective pain management and stress reduction strategy. Meditation improves memory and brain function, according to scientist Benjamin Neal. Teachers use meditation in the classroom to help their students focus and concentrate. Actors, artists, and innovators use meditation to help get themselves 'in the zone' and boost creativity.

Actors Tom Hanks, Cameron Diaz, Jennifer Aniston, and Kristen Bell all incorporate meditation into their daily routines. Authors Tim Ferris, Tony Robbins; comedians Jerry Seinfeld, Steve Harvey, and Ellen DeGeneres; and singers Katy Perry, Sheryl Crow, and Paul McCartney all use meditation to get ready for the day.

Oprah Winfrey spends at least 20 minutes each day meditating. She states that she is only capable of producing her best work when she is in a meditative state.

Meditation is one of the major keys to success. It gives you access to inspired ideas so that you can live your best life.

1. **Spend Time Reading:** The most popular item on a wealthy person's nightstand is a book. You will also find that many successful people have an entire library in their homes. Leaders are readers; if you want to increase your earnings, you've got to invest in learning. A successful person would rather spend $20 on a book than going to watch a movie for entertainment purposes. During an interview with CNBC, Warren Buffet and Bill Gates discussed what superpower they would like to have if it were possible. Their response was that they wanted to be able to speed read extremely fast.

Continuous education is one of the major keys to success—your personal development depends on it. If you are not learning, it's impossible to grow. Some people say they don't like to read or they don't have the time to read, but in this technological era, there is no excuse. Today, you can listen to audiobooks while you are driving, working, doing the dishes, or any other activity. If you've got a stack of gossip magazines sitting on your coffee table, it says a lot about your mindset. However, if you invest in books that will help you achieve your goals, your chances of success will significantly increase.

When you have been operating in the same bad habits your entire life, it can be difficult to break out of them. In the next chapter, you will learn some tips for building better habits to improve your self-discipline.

good opinoin

CHAPTER 6:

TIPS FOR BUILDING BETTER HABITS

The Navy SEALs are some of the most disciplined people in the world. It is extremely difficult to become a SEAL—admission requires strenuous training, and most soldiers who start the program leave before the end of the first stage. The soldiers who do complete it understand that the mind is more powerful than we can ever imagine. And because they have developed the mental fortitude required to succeed as a SEAL, they are equipped to accomplish any mission they are sent on. Here are some of the strategies the SEALs implement during training to get them through:

The 40 % Rule: Everything starts in the mind, if you lift weights at the gym, you know that after a certain number of reps, your body feels as if it can't continue. But the 40% rule states that when the mind starts telling the body it's tired, we have only reached 40% of what we are capable of. At this point, it's up to you to choose to believe that you've still got another 60% left in you. To push past the 40% threshold, you must accept the mental and physical pain you are enduring at that moment.

The majority of people never reach their full potential because as soon as they feel the burn, they are ready to give up. By applying the 40% rule, you begin to realize that you have unlimited potential. The key to tapping into this reservoir of potential is to ignore the voice in your head telling you it's time to throw in the towel, and push through the pain. When you truly believe you are capable of more, you will shatter your pain points, which builds confidence and mental toughness. For example, after doing ten pull-ups, you start hearing the voice in your head saying you are too tired, too weak, and too sore to keep going. But if you take a break for a few seconds and then keep going, you've just proved to the voice in your head that it was wrong! You then take another short break and do one more, and before you know it, you've done 20 pull-ups. You had to slow down to achieve it, but you ended up doing 20 more pull-ups than you had first anticipated.

Belief is one of the key ingredients to improving your self-discipline. Success becomes your reality when you believe you can do more, and it allows you to break down the limitations you have placed on yourself. Self-discipline is about endurance. When you are determined to continue but your mind is telling you to quit, you will build a resilience that will make you unstoppable.

The mind becomes our best friend when we believe in ourselves, but when we have accepted the narrative of failure, it becomes our worst enemy. The next time you feel like giving up, use the 40% rule to empower yourself.

I want you to take a moment and think about this: even though you know you are not fit enough because you haven't practiced, you decide to run a marathon. As you are running, your legs start feeling weak, you can't catch your breath, and at this point, you decide that running a marathon when you were not prepared wasn't a good idea. It probably would be wise to give up and save yourself the agony it would cause if you completed the marathon. But if someone wanted to cause you harm and you were running for your life, you would keep running regardless of how tired you were, because if you stopped, the person chasing you might kill you. The point is that most of us are ignorant of what we are really capable of. We have become complacent, we put on 10 lbs., buy a larger size, and convince ourselves that our stomach isn't protruding; or we work at a job we hate but the bills are getting paid, so we tolerate it. When we don't challenge ourselves, it is impossible to get a glimpse of our true potential. The people who master discipline have done so because they have chosen to be extraordinary. Outside of the excitement and camaraderie of watching sports, one of the reasons we love it so much is because we are admiring the players' ability to master their craft. If we were to invest the same amount of time we spent sitting in front of the TV watching other people display their expertise, we would probably be a lot farther ahead in life.

Several studies confirm that our physical abilities are determined by our mental strength. A popular study known as "the placebo effect" discovered that performance is enhanced when an individual believes they have done something to improve their performance. The *European Journal of Neuroscience* published a study in 2008, which found that participants who were told that the sugar pills they had been given were caffeine, put more effort into their weightlifting session. Due to the caffeine they believed they had ingested, they found additional strength and energy that allowed them to perform at a higher level.

Scientists agree that the placebo effect is a self-fulfilling prophecy, in which the brain chooses an outcome and then does what is required to make sure that the outcome is achieved. The placebo effect provides us with irrefutable evidence about the power of the mind. Several studies have also found that there is a chemical transformation in the brain when it thinks that something is real, even though it's fake. Therefore, it is enough to believe you've got another 60% left in you to make it possible.

Arousal Control: When we are in high-stress situations, large doses of cortisol and adrenaline are released, which activates the 'fight, flight or freeze' response. The average person is unable to control this process, but the Navy SEALs are capable of doing so because they have been trained to, and depending on the situation, their responses to stressful situations could mean the difference between life and death. They use several techniques to do this, including box breathing. When a SEAL starts feeling stressed or overwhelmed, they focus on their breath to regain control. They take a series of breaths for four seconds at a time—they breathe in, hold their breath, and then breathe out. This process is repeated until the heart rate returns to normal.

A stressed-out mind is incapable of doing anything productive; therefore, you must remain calm to operate at your full potential. Box breathing is a technique you can use at any time no matter where you are when you start experiencing the physical symptoms associated with anxiety. Experts often advise people to manage stress, but I don't think this is good advice when the Navy SEALs prove you can stop it altogether.

The 10 X Rule: Grant Cordone is the pioneer of the 10X rule. He believes we should set goals ten times higher than the desired outcome because it will make us take ten times more action to achieve it. The aim of the 10X rule is to force us to evaluate the way we think about our possibilities and the steps we are going to take to achieve our goals. Your current existence was created by your thoughts and actions, and if you want to overcome your limitations and start living the life you know you deserve, you must start thinking and acting in ways that are beyond your expectations. When using weight loss as an example, let's say your goal is to lose 10 lbs., apply the 10X rule and your goal is now 100lbs. Although you don't need to lose 100lbs, it will encourage you to change your diet permanently. The idea is that you don't need to do that much to lose 10lbs, which means the odds are increased that you revert back to your bad eating habits once you've lost the weight. However, when you have it in your mind that you need to lose 100lbs, you will focus on changing your diet and exercise habits as a lifestyle instead.

The 10X rule will maximize your potential. When you believe you can achieve more than you initially thought, you will do what is required to achieve more, which will strengthen your discipline. It's the norm for us to set low goals for ourselves so that we don't feel so worthless when we fail. But if you want to get more out of life, you are going to need to raise the bar and set your standards higher.

The 10 Minute Rule: You would assume that humans had better decision-making skills since we are far more mentally advanced than any other species. But a Harvard University study proves otherwise. The research involved giving chimpanzees and humans the same choice—to get two treats immediately or six treats in six minutes. The chimpanzees chose to wait for more treats seventy-two percent of the time, and the humans only chose to wait nineteen percent of the time. How did this happen? The problem is that the human brain is so overdeveloped that even when an answer is obvious, we overthink the decision. And because we have the ability to rationalize our behavior, we cheat ourselves out of a more favorable outcome. Humans tend to find it difficult to differentiate between a justification and an excuse. In the experiment, the humans may have convinced themselves that they deserved the treats because they were hungry and needed to satisfy their hunger, or that they weren't too concerned about getting six treats later because they didn't really like them anyway. Whereas the chimpanzees don't have the ability to rationalize their decision; they act on instinct and it's about survival of the fittest for them.

The ten-minute rule becomes effective at the rationalization stage. Let's say you are trying to lose weight and you decide you want a bag of chips, pause for ten minutes and then ask yourself if you still want the chips. If you decide you still want the chips, go ahead and eat them, or you can wait for another ten minutes since you've already managed to wait the first ten minutes. By choosing to wait, you eliminate the "immediate" from immediate gratification, enhance your decision-making skills and raise your discipline levels at the same time.

You can apply the 10-minute rule to a variety of situations. Let's say you are in the gym running on the treadmill and you start feeling tired. Instead of jumping off right away, keep running for another ten minutes and see how you feel. After doing it once, you will realize that you were not that tired after all and keep going.

There is nothing easy about discipline. We are not born with it, and all disciplined people develop it over time, including the Navy SEALs. Everyone has the ability to live a more disciplined life if they choose to. However, it is also important to note that there are some things that can hinder your self-discipline if you are not aware of them. I will discuss these in the next chapter.

CHAPTER 7:

WHAT IS HINDERING YOUR DISCIPLINE

Energy vampires are people who sap the life out of you with their negative attitude. But there are also things that can hinder your discipline and prevent you from becoming the best version of yourself. The majority of people understand that it takes discipline to get what you want out of life, so why is it that most of us are incapable of becoming disciplined enough to reach our full potential? I am not an advocate of the blame game, as I believe we should all take responsibility for our own lives. However there are some stealth ways that discipline can evade you without you realizing it. Maybe you are associating with the wrong people; you might have bad habits or crippling thought patterns you are not aware of. Your belief system about discipline might be wrong, or you may have the wrong motivations for what you want to achieve. The following factor may act as a hindrance to your discipline:

Parkinson's Law: If you tend to procrastinate, one of the excuses you might use is that you work best when you are under pressure. Parkinson's law validates this justification. A

British historian named Cyril Parkinson developed Parkinson's Law, which argues that when we have a set amount of time available, we will fill that time with the work. Parkinson started paying attention to the trend while employed by the British Civil Service. He noticed that as their bureaucracies increased, efficiency decreased. As employees were given more space and time, they took up more space and time. Parkinson noticed that even the most basic tasks were subconsciously made more challenging to fill the allotted time. However, when there was a tight deadline, they simplified the task to complete it faster.

If Parkinson's Law is hindering your discipline, you can overcome it by setting yourself tight deadlines for your tasks. When you give a project a time limit, you will find a way to get it done in the shortest amount of time, and you won't overcomplicate things to fill the additional time you have available. By setting yourself early deadlines, not only are you always challenging yourself, but you also put yourself under pressure to finish early, which frees you from the stress of rushing at last minute to meet deadlines.

Discipline Versus Procrastination: Procrastination hinders self-discipline; we convince ourselves that we are not taking action because we are waiting for the right time or the right circumstances. For example, you might decide to take a break from the gym because your legs are sore. On the surface, it sounds fair, but it's an excuse because you could still go to the gym and do cardio or work your arms instead. The core of self-discipline is doing what you need to do whether you feel like it or not. Inaction and making excuses are identical twins; there is no difference between them because they both lead to the same destination—failure. If you are going to wait until the conditions are just right, you've already lost the battle because when you want to do something, you are not stepping out of your comfort zone.

If you are making excuses now, you will keep making them in the future. The perfect circumstances don't exist—something is always going to be out of place. When procrastination seems logical, it's dangerous because it can apply to any situation. For example, if you decide you are going to quit smoking once there is less pressure at work, you will never give up because there is always going to be some level of stress at work. When you make excuses, you are telling yourself that you are not capable of doing what needs to be done now, but if you are incapable now, you are probably going to be incapable in the future.

You will always have doubts when you step out of your comfort zone. The excitement in challenges makes them attractive, but the fear of them can also convince you to abandon them. It's normal to doubt yourself when you are doing something you are not qualified for or when you are attempting to push your boundaries. But whether it's starting a business, writing a book, or improving your health, the right time to start is now, even if you don't feel that you are ready for it.

Another form of logical procrastination is spending too long on the planning stage when it comes to how you are going to achieve your goals. It is important to plan; however, there is no need to overanalyze things. The more time you spend planning means less time spent doing, which increases your chances of never getting started in the first place. The key is to start working on your project and figure out the details as you go.

Society also plays a role in our love-hate relationship with procrastination. The media encourages us to strive for perfection, whether it's in our marriage, place of employment, or social lives. This encourages procrastination because it's an impossible ideal to achieve. The fear of failure sets in and you keep postponing what you need to do to achieve your goals. You will push yourself into action when you realize that perfection and procrastination are both obstacles preventing you from becoming successful and disciplined.

A powerful technique that can be used to stop procrastinating and curb the desire for perfection is the seventy percent rule. The seventy percent rule states that you should get to work when you are seventy percent certain that you will succeed. One hundred percent certainty doesn't exist—you will never know whether something is going to work out unless you try it. The only way you are going to master discipline is through consistent action. So when you arrive at the seventy percent mark, decide that you are going to do it and stick to it. For example, you might want to compete in a marathon, but you know you are not fit enough. At your current state of athletic ability, you might be able to run two miles; that is your seventy percent and that's where you should start. As you train, you will keep building more strength, and before you know it, you are ready to run a full marathon.

False Hope Syndrome: False hope syndrome is the belief that it's easy to change your patterns of behavior. This leads to setting our expectations too high, which results in failure. Most of us have no idea how difficult it is to eliminate bad habits and assume that we are going to get everything we want out of life without facing a battle. False hope results in constant failure, which further reinforces the behavior we desire to change. Psychology Professor Peter Herman says that failure is more common than success, even though failure is never the goal. The reason for this is that we aim for extreme transformation that we are incapable of sustaining.

You might get momentarily inspired about your goals and map out a plan, but then the stresses of life take over, and that moment of inspiration fades into obscurity because your focus is on getting through the day and not on achieving a goal that's going to take you years to accomplish. If what you desire in life comes easy, it's not worth having. It takes time to achieve big dreams; there is no such thing as overnight success. Every successful person you see in the media experienced serious turmoil to get where they are today. All we see is the end result and assume that it was easy for them. Most people want success, but when they realize what it takes to achieve it, whether consciously or unconsciously, they bow out gracefully.

When you are evaluating the things that are hindering your discipline, take note of your actions. Are there any ways you are self-sabotaging? There is nothing pleasant about discipline, but we can also make it harder on ourselves. In the next chapter, you will learn about the importance of getting comfortable with being uncomfortable.

CHAPTER 8:

GET COMFORTABLE WITH BEING UNCOMFORTABLE

There is nothing comfortable about self-discipline. You don't need discipline to eat junk food or watch your favorite TV show because you enjoy doing those things. Unless they have a strong desire to achieve something, most people are not going to subject themselves to the discomfort of self-discipline. They are going to wake up just in time for work, eat when they are hungry, sleep when they are tired, etc. There is nothing you can do that is going to make self-discipline comfortable. We need endurance to overcome those feelings of discomfort, and mental toughness to plow through the instincts that are enticing us to choose the path of least resistance.

PRACTICE BEING UNCOMFORTABLE

In chapter one, you read about willpower being like a muscle that gets tired when it's used. But what this really means is that you can also strengthen your will power, which involves doing things on a regular basis that make you feel uncomfortable so that not only do you get familiar with the feeling of discomfort, but you get used to it. Stepping out of your comfort zone is important because it teaches you that your fears are not as great as you had imagined. One of the acronyms for fear is False Evidence Appearing Real, the evidence is false because you are imagining it, but you have turned that thought into a reality in your mind. The only way to dismantle this is to step into that fear and realize that the evidence you had conjured up in your mind was false. Every time you step out of your comfort zone, both your willpower and tolerance for discomfort will increase.

One of the most popular TED Talks came from Jia Jiang, in which he spoke about spending time living outside of his comfort zone. Jiang spent 100 days seeking out opportunities to experience rejection to help him overcome social anxiety and his fear of rejection to become a more confident person. It involved him doing things like asking a random stranger to lend him $100, knocking on someone's door and asking to play soccer in their backyard, and asking for second helpings in a restaurant without paying. At the end of the 100 days, Jiang was a completely different person—he was confident and sociable because of how kind people were to him during this time spent outside his comfort zone.

Jiang's story applies to all of us—our personal fears and discomforts are also opportunities to challenge ourselves. So, whatever you are comfortable with, do the opposite. If you are the more assertive type, act more passive throughout the day and vice versa. If you don't like speaking to strangers, go out and introduce yourself to people you don't know. If you can't dance, go to a dance class. There are plenty of things you can do to inject discomfort into your life.

One of the best ways to improve self-discipline is to get used to becoming uncomfortable. We all have different insecurities, fears, and discomforts, but most of us go through life avoiding them, which only limits our potential. If you want to become the best version of yourself, start by choosing to be uncomfortable and facing your fears.

As the practice of discomfort starts to build your willpower, you can start working on changing some of the habits and addictions that don't benefit you. Struggle and discomfort are a part of who you are. You decided to read this book because you want to become more disciplined, and if you want to succeed, becoming comfortable with discomfort will get you there.

The aim of this process is to turn that agonizing pain into a slight pinch and those hunger pangs into desire because it lets you know that you are sticking to your diet. Discipline is about going through the temporary discomfort required for the long-term benefits. Making a habit of embracing discomfort will benefit you in all areas of life. It will give you the mental agility required to thrive regardless of your circumstances. Discipline isn't concerned about your feelings—it doesn't care that you feel as if you can't take another step because that's when you need it the most. Practicing discipline is a brain training exercise, equipping it to default to perseverance mode.

URGE SURFING

There is no doubt that it is difficult to develop discipline, but there are ways to make the process easier. One of them is learning how to reduce the strength of temptations and urges. An urge is the physical and mental impulse to engage in habitual behavior.

The term "urge surfing" was pioneered by psychologist Alan Marlatt, an expert in the field of addiction. He compared urges to waves in the sea—waves rise up and down in intensity and eventually meet the shore and crash. What he was saying is that you have the ability to surf over those urges until they crash. Urge teaches you how to resist temptation and embrace discomfort. I want you to take a moment and think about an urge that you have recently experienced, think about how it made you feel physically and emotionally. Can you remember how those sensations evolved? As you are thinking about that urge, focus on your breath and imagine that the urge is a wave you are riding on.

It's the norm for us to identify with our urges, but urge surfing helps us separate ourselves from the bad habits we desire to correct. Instead of thinking, *"I feel like eating cake,"* say, *"I have an urge to eat a piece of cake."* In this way, you are not fighting yourself but the sensation you are experiencing, you can then allow it to pass. It's difficult to fight urges, but observing them without identifying with them increases your chances of overcoming them. The average urge will peak between 20 and 30 minutes if you fight with it. Fighting urges doesn't work because it makes them stronger and longer-lasting, which, in turn, diminishes your confidence about your ability to fight them.

You give your urges power through your willingness to indulge in them. There is actually no power in the temptations and the addictions. When a drug addict goes to a rehab facility and has no access to their drug of choice, they experience significantly few urges and cravings compared to when they are not in a rehab facility.

Another helpful way to define the internal struggle associated with urges is to think of it as a waterfall, and fighting an urge is like trying to block a waterfall. The waterfall is eventually going to break through with even more force than it would have originally because of the pressure that has been built up from being held back. Instead of trying to block the waterfall, step back and watch it.

If you can start seeing urges and temptations with curiosity rather than fear, changing your behavior will become a lot easier. Spend time studying your own habits and pay attention to your urges. Once you master urge surfing, you can overcome any addiction.

ARE YOU FEEDING YOUR URGES?

People will also do things like try to think themselves out of an urge or distract themselves so they are focusing on something else. This is similar to trying to fight your urges—they feed them, which makes them stronger. This then causes you to believe that the only way to get rid of your urges is to give in to them. When you get to this stage, you give up and accept that you will never be able to change your bad habits.

Distraction appears quite logical. After all, wouldn't it be better to limit the number of opportunities you have to engage in your bad habit instead of indulging in it? It sounds like a good idea in theory, but it doesn't work in practice. Several studies have found that suppressing thoughts, sensations, and feelings makes them stronger. To further prove this point, the next time someone mentions something, try not to think about it. For example, someone might say, "*Make sure you don't think about an elephant,*" now anytime the word "*elephant*" is mentioned, you are going to think about one and the more you try to avoid the thought, the more it will take over your mind. The same is true when you attempt to avoid urges. The aim of urge surfing is to leave you feeling calm and relaxed after walking away from a temptation—it's impossible to trick the mind into overcoming your urges. The only way out is to surf through the urge, which is a part of the discipline process. After a while, you will become comfortable with the discomfort of experiencing the urge and not submitting to it. Any time you feel an urge to do something you know is not going to benefit you, follow these steps:

- Pay attention to where the urge is coming from in your body. In the same way music gives you the urge to nod your head or tap your feet, the majority of urges are felt somewhere in the body.
- Once you have located where the urge is coming from, focus all your attention on that area and observe the sensations you are experiencing.
- Spend 2 minutes focusing on your breath.
- Imagine that every sensation and urge you are feeling is a wave. As the urge intensifies and subsides, look at it as a wave rising and falling.
- As the urge settles down, pay attention to the changes you are feeling.

Once you have surfed through an urge once, you will have the confidence to surf through them any time they arise. It's important to remember that urges are temporary. You are not going to feel that way forever—when you forget this, urges and cravings can become overwhelming. But if you have the confidence that you can ride through an urge, you will find that this method is much more effective than trying to fight with the urge or distract yourself. When you first experience hunger pangs, the assumption is that they won't go away until you eat something. As you probably know, you start feeling irritated when you're hungry because your productivity levels decrease. But people who fast know that hunger is temporary, it passes in the same way as every other urge. Most people start feeling hungry when they've been working for a while or when they get bored. But if you pay attention to what's going on inside your body, you will notice that your stomach isn't empty. If you spend a few minutes accepting the hunger and not looking at it as a sign that you need to eat immediately, the hunger will fade away quicker than you think.

Start paying attention to your urges, study them and experiment with them. You will find that the urges don't become a part of you until you start fighting with them or give into them. When you observe your urges from a distance and watch them coming and going, they lose their power to influence your behavior.

In order to reach your goals, you must develop a system to get you to your destination, and if you don't follow the right system, your dreams will never become a reality. In the next chapter, you will learn how to focus on the right system to get your desired outcome.

CHAPTER 9:

FOCUS ON THE SYSTEM

All successful people have goals. Yes, this is true—people set weight loss goals, financial goals, academic goals, relationship goals, but how many people actually achieve those goals? Research suggests very few people achieve their goals. There is nothing wrong with the goals they are setting, but there is something wrong with the system they are following.

When you set a goal, you are focused on the result you want to achieve, but a system is about the process you are going to undertake to get there. So, what would happen if you stopped focusing on the goal and focused on the system or strategy instead? For example, if a football coach wanted his team to win the championships but instead of focusing on winning, focused on the daily practice habits of the team, could they win? Probably. The only way to win is to improve your playing skills, and you can only do that through practice. If you want to win in life, forget about focusing on the outcome, focus on the system you are going to use to get to the outcome. Let me repeat, I am in no way stating that you shouldn't set goals; goals are necessary. If you don't know where you are going, how are you going to develop a system to get there? However, if you spend too much time looking at your goals without putting a system in place to get there, you are going to fall into that 80% of people who fail their New Year's resolutions each year.

WHAT DIFFERENTIATES THE WINNERS FROM THE LOSERS?

Everyone who competes in the Olympics wants to win, and everyone who goes to a job interview wants to get hired, so why is it that only one person gets the gold medal and only one person gets the job? The person who came second or third had the same goal, but they lost. What happened? The winner used the right system or strategy; the losers didn't.

GOALS DON'T LAST IF YOU DON'T CHANGE YOUR HABITS

Your bedroom has looked like a bomb has hit it for the past two months, so you set a goal to tidy it up, which you do, but in two weeks' time, it looks like a bomb has hit it again. Why? Because you have a bad habit of being untidy. You set a goal to lose 10 pounds, and you find enough motivation to go on a 30-day smoothie fast. You lose the weight, but in two months you've put it back on again. Why? Because you've got a bad habit of unhealthy eating. So, when the room gets messy again, and the weight returns, you'll be hoping to find the same level of motivation it took to do it the first time. This is a bad system and you will live your life continuously chasing outcomes if you don't change it. There is no point in taking Tylenol every time you get a headache. The headaches keep coming back for a reason and all you are doing is treating the symptom and not the cause. The cause may be that you don't drink enough water, and once you get into the habit of drinking enough water, the headaches will go away.

When you solve problems at the level of the result, you only get a temporary outcome. Once you resolve the inputs, the outputs will resolve themselves.

REACHING YOUR GOALS PUTS A LIMIT ON YOUR HAPPINESS

What do I mean by this? When you are on the other side of your goal you think, *"If I could just reach that weight, I'd be happy," "If I could just make enough money to buy a new house, I'd be happy."* Again, there is nothing wrong with these goals, but you are putting happiness off until you achieve the goal. You make happiness something that only the future version of yourself can enjoy. Additionally, goal setting creates an "either-or" conflict—you either achieve your goal and you're a success, or you don't and you're a failure. Life is full of ups and downs. You may get to your destination by taking a completely different route than you had planned, and that different route might take a lot longer than you had anticipated. This doesn't mean you are a failure, and neither does it mean that you can't give yourself permission to be happy. The only solution to this problem is to work from a systems-based approach, and as long as your system is running, you have the right to be happy because you know you are working toward your end goal.

THE YO-YO EFFECT

When all your energy is focused on reaching a particular goal, what do you have left to motivate you once you have achieved it? This is one of the reasons why people go back to old habits once they hit their target. This is referred to as the 'Yo-Yo Effect,' clinical psychologist from Yale University Kelly

Brownell coined the term during his research on obesity. He found that people who go on diets quickly put the weight back on once they've achieved their weight loss goal because they go back to their old eating habits instead of developing a system that will help maintain their desired weight. The same principle applies with goal setting in general. The main aim of setting a goal is to win the game, whereas the main aim of building a system is to keep playing the game. Life isn't about making single accomplishments, it's about continuous improvement and ultimately, it's your dedication to the process that will determine the extent of your progress.

The good news is that there is nothing wrong with you if you are finding it difficult to build good habits. The problem is the system you are using. Bad habits remain not because you don't want to change them but because you have adopted the wrong system. If your system is wrong, you will fail every time.

WHY YOU KEEP ON REPEATING BAD HABITS

We all know the feeling of starting a good habit only to fall back into our bad habits a few days later. It appears that the habits that are good for us like exercise, journaling, and meditation are great for a day or two and then they just become a burden. Bad habits seem to be a part of our DNA and there doesn't appear to be an end in sight. No matter how hard you try, unhealthy habits like smoking, eating junk food, procrastinating, and watching too much television seem impossible to overcome. There are two reasons why changing our bad habits is challenging: First, we focus on changing the wrong thing, and second, we focus on changing them in the wrong way. Let me break this down a bit further.

CHANGE IS COMPLEX

I think of change like an onion—there are several layers and each layer is unique in its own right. Here are three of the main layers of change referenced from 'Atomic Habits' by James Clear:

1. **The Result:** Whatever goal you set for yourself, you will expect a certain result. For example, you want to get the highest grade possible in your exams, you want to save a certain amount of money, or you want to start a business, etc.

2. **The Method:** Once you've set the goal, the next step is to come up with a system that will help you develop the habits required to achieve those goals. For example, if you want to get the highest possible exam results, you will need to develop a habit of consistent studying, and that means setting aside time to study every day.

3. **Who Are You?** The way you see yourself will determine your results because who you are is rooted in what you believe. The idea is that if you believe in something, you are going to live it out.

The method you use to reach your goals must be effective because it will make the difference between success and failure. Who you are manifests through your lifestyle. If a person claims to be a fitness guru, but their fridge is packed with junk food, that individual probably doesn't have the right belief system in place. They may want to be a fitness guru, but they haven't reached the point of living it out. Basically, it's not about focusing on the result, you need to focus on changing who you are so that don't fall into the trap of the yo-yo effect. Think about it like this, if two people have decided to quit eating junk food and they are invited out to their favorite fast food restaurant, one of them responds, *"Thanks for the offer, but I'm trying to stop eating junk food at the moment."* You can admire what the person is trying to achieve, but when you scratch the surface of their statement, what they are really saying is that they don't see themselves as a healthy person yet because they're still trying to stop eating junk food. On the other hand, the second person states in response to the fast food restaurant invitation, *"Thank you for the offer, but I don't eat junk food."* This statement is a lot more convincing because they have totally detached themselves from the bad habit of eating junk food. In other words, they've made the decision to change who they are. Because we live in fast paced microwave society where we are bombarded with the lure of immediate results, most people are unaware of the fact that sustaining any type of change requires a transformation in your belief system, you've got to change who you are first. People like Jennifer Lopez who have maintained amazing bodies throughout their career have done so not because of weight loss goals, but because healthy living is a part of who they are.

Your belief system will determine your actions. If you are a Christian and believe in Jesus, you are going to go to church on Sundays. If you are an athlete, you are going to practice with a coach several times a week. If your actions and your belief system are in conflict, you can expect failure.

ADOPT A NEW BELIEF SYSTEM

Another example found in the book Atomic Habits by James Clear, is about a man called Brian Clark who had a terrible habit of biting his nails. He was a successful businessman and had developed a nail biting habit during his childhood. It was a coping mechanism he had adopted any time he got nervous. His friends and family members didn't think his habit was healthy and encouraged him to stop biting his nails so they could grow. He summoned up every bit of willpower he could muster and stopped biting his nails. Being pleased with his efforts, Brian asked his wife to book him an appointment with a nail specialist, his thinking was that if he was paying to keep his nails looking good, he wasn't going to destroy them by nibbling on them. The technician made his nails look great, and she boosted his confidence even more by stating that he could have healthy nails if he stopped biting them. Brian left the salon with pride in the way his nails looked and he wanted to keep them that way. The only way he could achieve this was to stop biting his nails, initially, he set a goal to stop biting them until they were a little bit longer, but once he had the manicure and saw how good his nails looked he ditched his bad habit of biting them, and replaced it with the good habit of taking care of his nails.

You Are Your Habits

In his book Atomic Habits, James Clear also states that your habits determine who you are and they will be the deciding factor as to whether you achieve your goals or not. Once you see your bank balance growing, you will develop a habit of getting out of bed an hour early to work on your side hustle instead of sleeping in. Your desire to build your business will become stronger than your desire to get some extra sleep. When you start seeing the results that your good habits are producing, you will develop pride in your identity which will motivate you to maintain your good habits.

Any good habits you adopt will quickly fizzle out if they don't become a part of who you are. Motivation to see your desired outcome manifest is not enough. I will stress again that your good habits must become a part of who you are. Let's be clear, I am in no way advising you to stop setting goals, but your main aim should be to develop habits that will become a part of who you are for example:

- Set your goal to become a painter instead of someone who paints pictures in their spare time.
- Set your goal to become a good cook instead of someone who makes a gourmet dinner once a month.
- Set your goal to become an entrepreneur instead of just working on your side hustle to pay for a new car.

Everyone who drives knows that when they first started practicing, they had to calculate and think about every move. But now they drive unconsciously because it's become a part of who they are. The same is true of about your identity. Once you've developed the habit of healthy eating, you no longer need to will yourself to do it, it becomes second nature.

It is also important to mention that your identity can contribute to the limiting beliefs you have about yourself if you accept them as a part of your identity. For example:

- I don't spell very well
- I'm always speeding
- I hate learning new things
- I'm useless with technology
- I hate reading

The limiting beliefs you have about yourself are not facts, you can change them if you want to. It will be difficult because your subconscious mind has been programmed to keep you engaging in these behaviors. But with consistent effort, you can adopt the good habits required to change your identity for good.

There are going to be days when you've got to put your good habits on hold because you have other commitments; however, this is rare unless you have a serious emergency. When our bad habits become the norm, it is common to make the excuse that we are too busy to fit in good habits despite the fact that we have just spent a few hours scrolling through social media! Your identity will prevent you from forming good habits, and in order to make progress, you will need to spend time unlearning your current habits.

As well as the Navy SEALs, Zen Buddhists are some of the most disciplined people in the world. In the next chapter, you will learn about their philosophy and how they build self-discipline.

CHAPTER 10:

ZEN PHILOSOPHY AND GOAL ATTAINMENT

Wouldn't it be brilliant if you were able to cope with all life's major challenges and keep moving forward with a smile on your face? Wouldn't you like to live a life free from the anxiety we experience when things don't work out according to plan? What about letting go of the fear of not having done enough with your life? Or letting go of the fear of death? In this chapter, you are going to learn about the basics of Zen, an ancient philosophy that has enriched the Eastern lives for thousands of years. Its concepts will help you develop a greater level of self-discipline so that you can achieve your goals.

Over the last twenty years, researchers in the self-development field and psychology have been studying the superior psychological health of Zen practitioners. Researchers at Penn State University have spent the last ten years analyzing the effects of Zen practices. They have concluded that adding Zen practices such as meditation to your daily routine can reduce stress, help you make better decisions, and induce feelings of calm.

Zen Buddhists hold a reservoir of wisdom about accomplishing goals, overcoming fear, and delaying gratification. All of these actions provide a powerful foundation for self-discipline. Zen is not a religion—it is regarded as a life experience based on the teachings of Buddha. "Satori" is a Japanese term similar to Zen, meaning "flash of inspiration" or "first showing." To experience Zen, you must live in the present and have a deep belief that everything in the world is connected. To get a better understanding of Zen, gaining some insight into the life of Buddha will help.

THE LIFE OF BUDDHA

Thousands of years ago Buddha started to spread the observations and teachings that led to his enlightenment. His focus was on two main concepts—the first was that it was a natural part of human life to experience suffering. The second was that in most cases, we are responsible for the suffering we endure. Buddha departed from his life of luxury to get a better understanding of the world he was living in. He wanted to dig deeper into the concept of existence. He found that the majority of people were not happy. He eventually concluded that if we are going to reach the point where we believe that life has meaning, we must let go of self. We must let go of the idea that the world consists of "I" and "You," and accept that everything is interconnected. Once we have achieved this level of insight, the cares of this world such as acquiring material possessions and social status will no longer concern us. We can then begin to lead a much more balanced life by putting all our energy into moral development. We will also free ourselves from unnecessary suffering by relinquishing the idea that external events can make us happy.

LIVING IN THE PRESENT MOMENT

Buddhists believe that we should live in the present moment, and the past is nothing but a set of interpretations and memories. We have not yet entered the future, and so worrying and obsessing that things should turn out a certain way will only lead to unnecessary suffering. Next up are some examples from everyday life to help you put it into context.

Let's look at the issue of self-identity. Zen teaches us that the rigid ideas that we hold about who we are as individuals is self-limiting and keeps us bound to destructive behavior patterns. The first time I started reading about Zen, it dawned on me that the self-image I held was that of a high achiever. *"What's the problem with that?"* I can hear you asking. Well, if you know anything about what it means to be a high achiever, you will understand that it is a very difficult image to live up to and can wreak havoc on your mental health. When your life is spent being told by parents and teachers that you are intelligent and you are encouraged to keep on getting good grades, success becomes the main focus in your life. This starts from childhood and you carry the same mentality into adulthood. An immense amount of pressure is placed on you and you risk experiencing burnout and stress. You also become petrified of failure because you don't want to disappoint the people who are expecting you to succeed. You then begin working tirelessly every minute of the day to gain qualifications that you really don't care too much about. Each time you get a new qualification or accolade, does it give you permanent happiness? No, so what's the point?

If you do end up failing at something, your self-image is totally destroyed because all you have heard your entire life is that you are going to be successful. For high achievers, failure is a sign that you no longer have control over your life, and no one wants to feel as if their life is out of control.

ZEN PHILOSOPHY AND SELF-DISCIPLINE

So why will incorporating Zen principles into your life help you master self-discipline? First, you will accept that since there is no escape from suffering, you should prepare for it by working toward your goals. Second, you will have the ability to control your mind. Instead of wasting time and energy thinking about regrets and ruminating, you will focus on appreciating the present moment. Third, you will stop allowing fear to control you because fear is nothing but the result of thinking the worst about whatever situation you are in. If you learn how to stop focusing on negative possibilities, fear won't be able to dominate you. You will begin to think more clearly, and you will be much calmer because you are no longer battling with your negative thoughts.

Since Buddhism is all about living in the present, it only makes sense to question why you should even bother focusing on achieving your goals. However, the principles of Zen are not opposed to people becoming successful and accomplishing great things in life. Of course, you should plan for the future; only a fool would fail to do so. The idea is that you shouldn't live in fear concerning your future. Buddha put together a spiritual framework known as the Eightfold Path, and in it he provides guidelines about "right speech," "right view," and "right action." These guidelines are not only proactive, but they are also goals. The Eightfold path makes it clear that the principles of Zen are not opposed to goal attainment. When you live in the present, you think about the small steps you can take to achieving your goals instead of focusing on the fact that you are so far from where you want to be. When you don't live in the present, it is easy to start feeling demotivated when you look at your current situation and start thinking about what you don't have. It makes the journey ahead seem so much longer. The question then becomes: how can you train yourself to start thinking like a Zen Buddha?

HOW TO MASTER SELF-DISCIPLINE THE SHAOLIN WAY

Now that you have a better understanding of the main principles of Zen, it's time to look at the lifestyles and habits of some of the most disciplined people on the planet—Buddhist monks—the Shaolin.

By analyzing the monks' everyday beliefs and routines, you will begin to understand how applying the principles outlined above can set the foundation for a life of self-discipline. So, who exactly are these people who have mastered self-discipline in such a profound way? One of the most well-known Zen Buddhist temples in the world is the Shaolin Monastery in China. History states that it was founded around 1500 years ago when a Buddhist teacher called Bugghabhadra arrived in China from India. He decided that Buddhist teachings should be passed down from master to student. Prior to this, Buddhist monks had typically relied on written interpretations and scriptures. The Chinese Emperor was very impressed with Bugghabhadra's idea, and as a result, provided him with the finances to build the temple. Not only were the monks trained in spiritual matters, but they were also trained in martial arts, and to this day are known for their superior fighting skills. They are taught a series of special moves including the "Iron Head" technique. Monks who have perfected this move are capable of breaking a slab of concrete with their forehead. The monks have become such experts that they often travel around the world to showcase their skills to large audiences. Despite several demolitions and attacks throughout history, monks still reside in the temple.

The monks start their day at 5 am, and it ends at 11 pm, and during this time, they participate in three main activities. Essential temple activities such as preparing food and cleaning, kung fu, and the study of Buddhism. All monks spend several hours throughout the day practicing grueling exercises, as well as undergoing intense spiritual and mental training. They are restricted from having outside interests and they own very few material possessions. When a monk joins the temple, they must shave their head to pledge allegiance to Buddha teachings and to demonstrate that they are willing to relinquish their attachment to material possessions.

So, what is the Buddhist monks' secret to such a high level of self-discipline? Matthew Ahmet is a British-born monk who spent several years training at the temple. He discovered that the Shaolin have a very different attitude than westerners. First, the monks live with the most basic facilities, they do not have access to running water and they wash their clothes by hand. This makes them extremely grateful for the small things in life. When you can appreciate the small things, it is good for your mental health. You start to feel that the world is a good place to be in and that it has an abundance of opportunities. This encourages you to achieve your goals. Second, the monks believe that wealth and material possessions will not make you happy. They do not envy those who live normal lives because during their training they learn that true happiness comes from finding your mission or passion. In their case, it's the physical and spiritual progress they make while they are at the temple. This lesson is simple, but it is extremely powerful. When you find a goal that aligns with your ambitions and values, your passion will be the vehicle that carries you. Even when the challenges of life begin to bombard you and you start paying attention to how far you've got to go to achieve your goal, the fact that you have a purpose in life will keep pushing you onward.

Third, they don't believe in pushing themselves to the point of injury or pain. In the past, the monks had to be physically fit and ready to defend themselves at all times in case there was an attack on the temple. They believed that a monk who was injured or ill because of too much mental or physical exertion would be incapable of defending the temple. The same attitude is held by the temple inhabitants today. Even though the monks spend many hours in physical training, they also take the time out to relax. They understand that you don't need to be busy to be productive. The monks are taught that to avoid burn-out, you need to slow down. This is one of the reasons why they meditate. According to Ahmet, this is the most effective way of building psychological strength, reducing mind chatter, and learning how to balance downtime with hard work.

The monks spend several hours per day meditating. Kung fu practitioners believe that it's important to have control over your emotions so that you are not dominated by negative impulses. To be an efficient fighter, you must learn how to harness your essential life force. The word "chi" is how the Shaolin tradition describes this concept. In Chinese, the word "chi" means "temper," "air" and "energy." Monks spend several years training in kung fu and Tai chi. Tai chi requires an extreme amount of balance and concentration to perform the moves. The original aim of Tai chi was to teach fighters how to remain focused and aware in the moment in case they need to strike. Shaolin monks claim that their ability to remain so resilient and resistant in the face of injury is because of their mastery of chi. Monks are capable of withstanding fatal blows to the abdomen and internal organs. This is achieved by redirecting their energy so that blows are repelled, and they remain uninjured.

As well as giving you the ability to quiet your mind and master your chi, meditation also helps you to get in touch with your inner person. When it comes to discovering your purpose and passion, meditation is the most important step. Shaolin monks do not experience the pain of not wanting to get out of bed in the morning. They wake up with energy and excitement because they know what they want to achieve in life. They are driven to mental, physical, and spiritual excellence because of this inner conviction. For Shaolin monks, meditation is a way of life; they don't view it as a practice or as a single experience. They aspire to operate at the highest level of concentration at all times and to live a life of continual mindfulness. If you have read the chapter about the Navy SEALs, you can see how much they have in common with Shaolin monks. They are exceptionally disciplined, and they are willing to give up short- term comforts for attaining long term goals.

Although the lifestyle of Shaolin monks is profoundly different from the average person, they do have one thing in common with productive people—they stick to a daily routine (such as those in chapter five). So, you've read a lot about meditation—in the next chapter, you are going to learn how you can start using this powerful spiritual practice to improve your self-discipline.

CHAPTER 11:

MEDITATION FOR SELF-DISCIPLINE AND FOCUS

In the last chapter, you read about how important meditation is for improving self-discipline. In this chapter, you will learn a few basic exercises that will help improve your meditation skills. Some people might not be interested in meditation because they assume it's a boring practice that involves you sitting cross-legged for hours at a time humming! This is a totally false assumption. First of all, you don't need to remain seated for hours to meditate. Second, meditation is a lifestyle and not a practice, and that is the attitude you should have about it. Before going into specific meditation techniques, let's take a look at how it's going to benefit you.

THE BENEFITS OF MEDITATION

- Meditation increases your ability to concentrate and focus on the task at hand. It also boosts your capacity to make rational decisions. It will improve your ability to delay instant gratification so that you can focus on what you want in the long term. The challenges of everyday life are not going to disappear, but you will develop the ability to handle them better.

- Meditation gives you the ability to respond to the most tragic circumstances of life with a rational and calm outlook.

If you are still feeling skeptical about meditation, there is plenty of scientific evidence highlighting the benefits of the practice. The journal *PNAS* published a study stating it takes approximately seven days to start experiencing results from meditation. The study involved getting 40 undergraduate students to participate in 20 minutes of meditation training for five days. During this time, they were given several psychological tests, and results found that they were less anxious, less stressed, and less tired than the control group.

Think about how your productivity would improve if you had more control of your thoughts and you had more energy? Even when you are not motivated to do what needs to be done, the skills you learn through meditation will push you through. And this is what self-discipline is all about.

MEDITATION TECHNIQUES

Before you begin, read these instructions over a few times so you are familiar with them and won't need to keep breaking your concentration to go back to the book and find out what you need to do next.

THE JUST SITTING TECHNIQUE

This seated meditation technique is referred to as "Zazen." Shaolin monks practice it often, and it involves you sitting comfortably. You can sit upright on a chair, sit with your legs crossed on the floor, or adopt the lotus position if you wish. If you don't want to fall asleep during the process, it's not advised that you do this in bed. Sleep is a good thing; however, in order to reap the full benefits of meditation, you need to stay awake. Once you have found a comfortable position, keep your back straight, but make sure it isn't rigid. Don't clamp your mouth shut, but keep it closed, keep your eyes open but don't stare, your gaze should remain soft and focused on the floor around two feet in front of you.

Once you are in the correct physical position, the next step is to focus on the mind. There are two different techniques—you can try them both and see which one suits you the best. Start by paying attention to your breathing. This silences the chatter in your mind and forces you to remain in the present moment. As you inhale and exhale, feel the way the air moves through your nostrils and mouth. Don't breathe from your chest, breathe from your stomach. In the West, we practice shallow breathing from the chest, this limits the flow of oxygen and causes us to feel tired. Buddhists believe it is important to practice proper breathing because it allows a good flow of energy through the body. Proper breathing has several health benefits. If you suffer from panic attacks and anxiety, it can be very helpful to learn how to control your breathing. Inhaling slowly through the nose and out through the mouth balances oxygen levels in the body, which will make you feel better.

THE SHIKANTAZA TECHNIQUE

The second technique is referred to as "Shikantaza," which means "just sitting." This exercise is slightly more challenging than the one described above, so don't get discouraged if you feel that it's not working out for you after a few attempts.

Sit and pay attention to what is going on around you and within you. Most people find that their mind is full of noise when they practice this. When you sort through the information going through your mind, you will realize that you carry around a lot of junk. However, the aim here is not to judge yourself about the things you are thinking about, but to acknowledge each thought, and then let it go. Envision your thoughts as clouds floating along in the sky. You can't get them to disappear, but you can watch them as they pass you by, instead of focusing on what they mean. Once you learn how to do this, your negative thoughts won't have such a bad effect on you, and you will be able to let them go and redirect your energy toward things that are more productive. Not only will you be a more positive and happier person, but you will also stop wasting time on behaviors that don't serve you. You will begin to feel empowered as you take control of your mind.

Whether you are "just sitting," or focusing on your breath, your mind will start wandering, you will have thoughts such as, *"This is stupid, why am I wasting my time?"* or *"I think too much; I will never be able to empty my mind."* Don't allow yourself to get caught up in the mental chatter. As soon as you realize that you have lost control of your thoughts, try to focus on the present again. Don't start condemning yourself for it because you will invite more mental chatter, and that is what you are trying to get rid of. Meditation is a skill, and the more you practice it, the better you will become at it. If you've been living the fast-paced Western lifestyle for your entire life, don't expect to achieve inner peace overnight. However, as the research states, you should start to feel in control of your emotions and life, and a lot calmer within seven days of consistent practice.

If you find it difficult to sit still for more than a few minutes, or you suffer from such severe anxiety that you find it unbearable to sit and confront your thoughts, try "Kinhin," a form of Zen walking meditation. Start by removing your shoes and socks, and then stand up straight but don't stiffen your back. Stand firm without rocking back and forth on your feet, your weight should be evenly distributed, and you should feel grounded. Draw your thumb toward your palm and then wrap your fingers around your thumb. Lightly place your hand against your stomach just above your belly button. Position your right hand over the top of your left hand, gaze at the floor about six feet in front of you. Your gaze should be concentrated but soft.

Take one step forward with your right foot. Each time you breathe in and out, take one step forward. As you walk, aim for slow, controlled movements in a clockwise direction. It will take an incredible amount of self-discipline to keep an even pace. This is an excellent way of developing self-control. Every time you complete the meditation, you prove to yourself that you have the ability to master your movements. This translates into a more proactive, stronger, mental attitude that will benefit every area of your life.

When developing good habits, the aim is to start small and then scale up. Therefore, it is advised that you start with 10 minutes a day—five minutes in the morning and five minutes in the evening. From now on, make meditation a non-negotiable part of your life. Don't "try" to meditate, just do it. The word "try" is a recipe for disaster; in the next chapter, I will tell you why.

CHAPTER 12:

WHY YOU SHOULD NEVER "TRY AND DO" ANYTHING

One of the most helpful things you can do right now on your journey to improved self-discipline is to remove the word "try" from your vocabulary. This minor change will transform the way you see yourself and boost your self-esteem. The way you think is not the only thing that shapes your life. Your words have power whether you say them out loud or in your head—they influence the way you see yourself and how far you succeed. In this chapter, you will learn how the word "try" can hold you back from achieving your dreams and put a limit on your self-discipline.

STOP TRYING YOUR BEST

As children, we are encouraged to try our best. Well-meaning teachers and parents tell children that as long as they try their best, the end result doesn't matter. Popular sayings such as, *"At least you tried"* or *"It's the taking part and not the winning that's important,"* further reinforce this attitude. It is a comfortable sentiment because it suggests that there are always going to be other opportunities to succeed. The reality is that there are going to be times when you won't get another chance to make it right. You've got to capture that moment because you will never get it back.

From this day forward, you are not going to TRY, you are going to DO! You must be decisive and have courage in everything you say and do. As a result, you will start to respect yourself more, and so will other people. They will regard you as a proactive winner instead of someone who does nothing because they are afraid to fail. When you have made up your mind that the only thing you can do is try instead of expecting to succeed, you are accepting that you are putting a limit on what you are capable of achieving. There are times when fate will be on your side, and you will achieve what you set out to with the "try" mindset; however, as a general rule, life will give you exactly what you give to it, and when you take action instead of just trying, you will always get better results.

There are different shades of gray to try. This means that when you aim to "try" instead of "do," you are less likely to hold yourself accountable. When you operate with a "try" mindset, you give yourself plenty of room to give up as soon as you feel that you've done enough. How hard will you "try" until deciding that you have done enough? Your effort is difficult to measure, isn't it? This opens the door to self-deception because now you can tell yourself that you've "tried," even though you've made minimal effort. On the flip side of this, when you actually "DO," the evidence is there for you and others to see. It's simple—did you go ahead and get the job done or not? Excuses have no residence in the "DO" mentality. If you want to see results, you've got to be self-disciplined.

BECOME A DOER

When you are a "DOER," you've got to trust in yourself and your abilities; but at the same time, you've got to be realistic. For example, if you need to lose 100 lbs., don't expect to lose the weight because you worked out and dieted for one month. Take an honest inventory of your strengths, weaknesses, and skills. Taking inventory of what you are capable of is an act of self-discipline in itself because it takes courage to confront yourself in this way. Don't waste time indulging in a "poor me" attitude—this isn't going to get you moving in the direction of your goals. If you know that you have what it takes to succeed, go out there and get it done. If you want to achieve something that is going to require help from others who are more knowledgeable than you, ask for help. If you need to acquire a new skill set, go out and get whatever qualifications you need to turn the dream you have into a reality.

It is also important that you have total belief in yourself and that what you are doing will help you accomplish your goals. You will need to put in a lot of effort and spend plenty of time reflecting on yourself, your life, and the direction you are heading. However, by this point, you will have accepted that the only way to achieve anything of value is through hard work and dedication. Before you start working on a new project, make sure you are fully aware of what you want to achieve. Thinking about it is not enough—get a pen and notepad and write it down. If you are unsure of your aims, delay getting to work until you *are* sure because, if you don't know where you are going, you will end up wasting a lot of time and energy. Also, when you fail to plan, failure is inevitable. You run the risk of developing a reputation as someone who is always starting new ventures and never completing them. You then get trapped in a vicious cycle that ultimately will erode your self-esteem and confidence. There is only one solution to this problem—choose your goals according to your abilities. Once you are confident that you can succeed, go for it. "Trying" is a recipe for disaster, whereas "doing," is decisive and assertive.

Trying leads to unhelpful, negative beliefs that will prevent you from achieving your goals. For example, let's say you want to lose 20 lbs. and you say that you will "try" to workout throughout the week and you will "try" to stick to your new diet. Through the words you have spoken, you have already set yourself up for failure. When you set out to "try," what you are saying is that you are not confident you can do this, and you get stuck thinking about what will happen if you don't hit your target. The more you focus on the things you don't want, that is what you will attract into your life. When you have decided that this is what you are going to "do," you will begin to envision the slimmer version of yourself wearing swim shorts or a bikini and feeling attractive and confident.

SET REALISTIC GOALS AND BELIEVE IN YOURSELF

Successful people understand that if they are going to achieve their goals, they must believe they will succeed, and keep pushing themselves harder. Instead of "trying," they "do." For example, one of the most successful self-development experts in the world, Deepak Chopra, is well known for his high energy levels and productivity. At 73 years of age, he is still traveling the world giving speeches. When asked how he manages to keep building his publishing empire despite the number of other demands he has in his life, one of his responses has been, *"Don't try, Do."*

Apart from eliminating words such as "try" from your vocabulary, how else can you change your mindset from a person who "tries," to someone who "does?" You can start by setting goals for yourself that you know you will accomplish. For example, saying you will spend five minutes per day exercising is achievable, and will give you the confidence that self-discipline is a realistic possibility for you. Positive self-talk is also an important factor in this process. Once you have set yourself a realistic goal, remind yourself several times throughout the day that you are going to DO it.

Also, when you are confident about the direction you are heading in and how you are going to get there, you are more likely to arrive at your destination because you have a clear idea of where you want to go. In the next chapter, I am going to speak about the habits of winning and losing—no one wants to lose, and everyone wants to win. However, your habits will determine which category you fall into.

CHAPTER 13:

WINNER OR LOSER, WHICH ONE ARE YOU?

I f you are confused about what goals to set for yourself, start with deciding that if you don't do anything else in life, you will reach your full potential. You will find that to reach your full potential, you need a combination of self-awareness and self-discipline. Even when we are doing nothing, life never stands still. It is an ever-changing and dynamic experience, and you will only start to live your best life when your perception of life changes. Life is a training academy—we are always learning and always growing. Your education shouldn't stop because you've graduated from college or high school. When you sit still for too long, you run the risk of losing momentum. There is no "opt-out" clause in life—you are either practicing going in the winner's direction or the losing direction. Which direction you choose to take is up to you, nobody can make that choice for you. In this chapter, we will cover five basic rules that will equip you to excel in every area of your life. Whether you want to lose some weight, find a loving relationship, or become more efficient at work, these principles will help you do so. Once you have mastered these strategies, not only will your productivity rise to new levels, your confidence and self-esteem will too. A quick reminder, there is nothing easy about success—if you don't put the work in, you will fail no matter how much knowledge you've acquired.

Know What You Want: Have you ever gotten into a car and attempted to get to a destination you were unfamiliar with? You are probably thinking, why would anyone do that? You are correct, in this day and age, with all the technology we have access to, all it takes is for you to type the zip code into your mobile device and it will direct you there. Knowing where you are going is crucial to your success. If you don't know, like the driver in a car making his way to an unfamiliar destination, you will end up going around in circles, wasting time trying to find out whether certain paths will lead to your destination. The more detail you add to your goal, the easier it is going to be for you to achieve it. You need something that is going to light a fire up in you. Think about these two statements, *"I'm going to lose 20lbs"* or *"I'm going to lose 20lbs, triple the amount of weight I can lift at the gym, and save some money to buy two new outfits once I achieve my goal."* Which of these statements are you most excited about? The second one is more inspiring because it is specific and incites emotion. Humans are driven by emotion—we need to feel something before we act.

When deciding what you want, you also need to consider your 'why?' Pursuing a goal for the sake of it is not going to get you out of bed in the mornings. Why do you want to achieve this goal? Everything you set out to accomplish should line up with your core values and ultimate purpose in life. For example, you might have a goal to write a 100,000-word book about how you overcame depression. To the average person, this sounds like an impossible task, but you know it's something you can achieve because you have a passion to help others get out of the trap of depression and you know it's possible. It is this end vision that will motivate you to get out of bed in the morning or come home from work and start typing instead of turning on the TV. Your 'why' is the vehicle that will push you in the direction of success.

You should also think about the things you will need to sacrifice to get you to your final destination. Remember, there is no escape from pain and suffering, and this is also true when it comes to achieving your dreams. If you are going to achieve anything worthwhile in life, you will need to give up something. For example, if you want to meet a certain financial goal, achieving it might require that you get a second job and stick to a strict budget. If you want to lose weight, you will need to wake up earlier and work out. When you are setting your goals, think about the things you will need to give up so that you don't get disheartened along the way. Furthermore, taking into consideration the things you will need to give up will help you decide whether the goal you want to achieve is really worth the sacrifice.

Give it Your Best Shot: You know when you've tried your best and when you've only put 50% effort into achieving your goals. Let's say you're studying for an exam, you are aiming to get the highest grade possible, so you establish a routine and don't waiver from it. You sit the exam, your results come, and you get the highest grade. Let's say instead of sticking to your timetable, you spend most nights watching Netflix and playing computer games. When the results come, your grade is below average. Deep down, you know you've got no one else to blame but yourself. There were no extenuating circumstances, you simply failed to honor your word. Discipline demands that you do what needs to be done even when you don't feel like it. When you train yourself in this way, success is inevitable.

Don't Make a Big Leap: It takes just as much self-discipline to take small strides toward your goal as it does to take huge strides. When you first start making your way to your destination, it's tempting to try to get there as quickly as possible by taking huge strides. When you think about it, it sounds like a brilliant idea. You get all excited and you experience an initial burst of energy that makes you feel as if you can take on the world, so you put all your energy into making progress. But you will soon find that motivation runs out, and we also need more than motivation to achieve our goals. The solution to this problem is to make a plan and follow it to the letter. May I add that there's nothing wrong with feeling excited and motivated; after all, if you are not going to be excited about achieving your goals, who is? However, the easiest way to achieve a goal is to work toward it at a measured and sensible pace; keep a journal and use it to monitor your progress. Once you have arrived at your destination, you can look back at where you've come from and feel proud of what you've achieved.

Repetition is the Key to Success: Let's say you have a goal to become fluent enough in Spanish that you can read a Spanish newspaper without struggling. Your first step in achieving this goal would be to work out what drills and exercises you will need to help you master the vocabulary, grammar, and spelling of the Spanish language. You might need to download a few apps, buy some books, or pay for some lessons. Your next step is to commit to repeating those exercises every day. There is nothing fun about repetition, but it is one of the requirements for success. Sometimes, you are going to feel frustrated because it seems as if you are not making any progress. You might miss a day every now and then, and that's fine, just make sure you pick up where you left off and decide that you are going to re-commit to this goal moving forward. Don't waste any time making excuses or beating yourself up over it.

Celebrate Your Wins: For example, if your goal is to run a full marathon and you are out of shape and haven't exercised in years, it's going to seem like an impossible task. However, the trick is not to focus on the end goal, or you will end up feeling disappointed and might give up altogether. Focus on reaching small milestones and celebrating every time you achieve one. So, you could celebrate every time you are able to run two miles nonstop, the next would be five, then ten, etc. The more you win, the more you will start to see yourself as a winner.

Whatever goal you want to accomplish, remember, what you choose to focus on is what you will attract. As long as you take consistent action and believe in yourself, you will achieve it. In the next chapter, I will tell you why it's essential that you find it exciting to chase your goals.

CHAPTER 14:

FALL IN LOVE WITH THE PROCESS

Once you know what goal you want to achieve, and you've developed a plan to get there, the next step is to enjoy the process. A lot of people get excited about finding their passion, setting goals, and putting a system in place, but when the reality of the amount of work that is required to achieve their goals sets in, they give up. The problem is that human beings don't like stepping outside of their comfort zone; in fact, the body is designed to operate in this way. Unless you were raised in a family where success was mandatory, and you were trained from childhood to develop good habits, you will find the process of goal setting very difficult. If you study the most successful athletes in the world, you will discover that the majority of them have been training since childhood. For example, before anyone knew who the Williams sisters were, their father started training them to become professional tennis players at the age of three. We saw Venus win her first professional match at the age of 14, that's 11 years in training! Christiano Ronaldo is regarded as one of the world's greatest soccer players, he started training at the age of 11! Tiger Woods has been learning to play golf since the age of 6! The point I am trying to make is that excellence is not birthed overnight. You are not going to write out your goals and achieve them tomorrow, it's going to take some serious hard work on your part.

If you are going to make the transition from setting goals to achieving them, it's essential that you learn to enjoy the process no matter how difficult it is. Why? Because if you attempt to rely on determination and motivation to get you through, you will give up before you've even started building momentum. In this chapter I will teach you how to change the way you think about hard work and start enjoying the process of success.

THE POWER OF ASSOCIATION

There are limitations to motivation. You feel empowered when you focus on your goals, but the daily grind of getting you there will completely drain your energy unless you learn to enjoy the work involved. The good news is that with some basic knowledge of psychology, you can start getting just as excited about the journey as you are about the destination.

Have you ever trained an animal? If so, you will have some knowledge about the power of association. Psychologist Ivan Pavlov demonstrated this in the 1890s with a study he conducted on the way dogs salivated when they were fed. After some time, he noticed that the dogs would salivate when they heard the footsteps of Pavlov's assistant or when he walked into the room, even if he wasn't carrying any food. Pavlov concluded that the dogs associated mealtime with the sound of footsteps, which triggered an automatic salivation response. He investigated this further and introduced a bell to feeding time; Pavlov began to ring a bell just before mealtime and within a few days, the dogs had formed an association with the sound of the bell ringing and mealtime. They would salivate at the sound of a bell even if there was no food.

What relationship does Pavlov's experiment have with 21st-century humans? It demonstrates that instead of having to force certain responses, we can make the process a lot easier by using the power of conditioning. If you can pair an unpleasant or difficult task with positive feelings, over time, you will start to enjoy the task because a positive association of action and feeling has been formed in your mind. What I am saying is that it is possible to feel happy at the thought of hard work! It might sound too good to be true, but to make it even better, the process is relatively simple and easy to accomplish. Your only job is to think about how you can trigger feelings of calm and pleasure before, during, and after you have completed a task. May I stress that even though this is a simple process, the only reason people fail is because they are not consistent. Conditioning doesn't happen overnight, and if you are not willing to put the work in over the short term, you will not reap the long-term benefits. Let's take a look at how this can work for you on a personal level.

Let's say you want to launch your own company, but you need to put a business plan together to apply for a bank loan. You know that this will take several hours of research and then additional hours of research to put the plan together. The idea of sitting in front of your laptop to accomplish this goal fills you with dread and so you keep putting it off. What can you do to form a positive association with this difficult task? Here are some ideas to get you started.

How to Form Positive Associations

Think about your favorite snack or beverage—before sitting down to start working on the business plan, you prepare your snack or pour out a cup of the drink you like. After a while, your mind will begin to associate the act of consuming your favorite drink or snack with working on your business plan. Or you can spend a few minutes listening to your favorite motivational speaker or reading an inspirational article before you start work. Or you might enjoy taking a hot shower with a scented shower gel. This will encourage you to associate a certain smell and temperature with productive work.

While working, play some light music in the background to keep you motivated. People generally find that music with lyrics is too distracting, but go on YouTube and type in "productivity music" and you will find a selection of playlists that will help keep you focused while working. After a while, you will begin to associate this music with productivity and a self-reinforcing cycle will set in. After each session, give yourself a reward to congratulate yourself for getting through the process. For example, you can watch an episode of your favorite TV series, or you can read a few chapters of the fiction novel you've been so excited about. There is a lot more to creating a system of rewards then giving yourself a pat on the back. What you are doing is training your brain to create a link between hard work and positive emotions. If you are consistent with this routine, you will eventually get to the point where the process will become so automatic that you won't need the reward. You will have developed such a strong association with the reward that your hard work will be its own payoff.

Here is another example, maybe you want to start going to the gym more often because you want to lose some weight. You could create a playlist of your favorite songs and listen to them while working out. This will give you an incentive to go to the gym, and as the association with your favorite music and going to the gym intensifies, the idea of working out will become more exciting to you. You will begin to find the mere thought of going to the gym pleasurable, so that even if you forget your playlist, you will still enjoy the experience.

Repetition is the key to success. When you repeat an action over and over again, you will stop wasting your time and energy debating whether you should or shouldn't participate in the action required to achieve your goal—it will become as natural as brushing your teeth, and you will just do it.

Another powerful technique that can assist you in learning to love the process of goal attainment is to associate your success with your identity. What do I mean by this? Think about the type of person you will become once you have achieved your goal in comparison to the person you are now. At present, you might feel a little bit insecure because you are not where you want to be in life. Maybe you are overweight, or you are not earning the money you would have hoped to be earning at this age. Thinking of yourself as a person who is making a transition from the person you are now, to the person you aspire to become will encourage you to keep pushing as you work hard to achieve your goal. With every milestone you achieve, your new identity will become more realistic as each day passes.

If your goal is to run a full marathon, don't see yourself as someone who is working toward achieving this goal, but see yourself as someone who is health conscious, full of energy, and for whom exercise is a part of life. Remember, your thoughts are powerful. The more time you spend thinking about something, the more you will attract it into your life. How do you want to feel about yourself? Would it encourage you to know that the only thing standing in the way of you and the person you want to become is consistent action? A clever way to think about the process of hard work required for progress toward your goals is to feel grateful for having the opportunity to improve your life. So many people are caught up in the stresses of life that they have no time to sit down to even think about the better life they want to live, let alone start taking the required steps to achieve that dream life. Just before you start working on a project, or you are about to start that workout session, take a few minutes to think about how grateful and excited you are to have this amazing opportunity to change your life. You can also implement a gold star reward—there is a reason why they did this in school. Do you remember how excited you got after handing in an assignment and getting it back with a gold star and a *"Well done"* at the end of the project? Not only were you proud of yourself, but it also encouraged you to put your best efforts forward so you would get another gold star you could run home and tell mommy about.

Sticking gold stars on a calendar for each day that you went to the gym might sound like something you would do only in elementary school, but seeing those gold stars will fill you with a sense of achievement and empower you to keep moving toward your end goal. If you are going to implement this strategy, hang the calendar up at a location where you will see it every day, so that every time you look at it and you are reminded of your achievements so far, you are encouraged to keep going, even if you still have a long way to go.

As well as learning to enjoy the process, you will also need to train yourself to view your negative emotions in a positive light. Negative emotions are a fact of life, and there is a good chance you will experience them, even more so while you are working to achieve your goals. However, once you change your perception of negative emotions, they will begin to work for you and not against you. I will discuss this process in the next chapter.

CHAPTER 15:

HOW TO MAKE YOUR NEGATIVE EMOTIONS WORK FOR YOU AND NOT AGAINST YOU

No matter how positive you are, or how close you are to achieving your destiny, feelings of sadness, despair, anger, and frustration will engulf you at some point. To be human means to experience a full spectrum of emotions, and that includes the good and the bad. It is natural to want to protect ourselves from anything negative, and so when we are not feeling our best, we will attempt to shut out those feelings as quickly as possible. In this chapter, I am going to share with you the reality that not only is it healthy to embrace your negative emotions, but when it comes to operating in your purpose and becoming more disciplined, they are extremely beneficial.

As long as you have learned to accept the fact that you will never escape suffering in this lifetime, you are ready to benefit from unpleasant emotions. Negative emotions such as despair and sadness are an indication that something is not quite right, and it needs to change. Don't think of your negative emotions as an inconvenience that needs to be removed from your life;

instead, view them as helpful signposts leading you in the direction of positive change. Use your negative emotions as an incentive to construct a plan of action to get you out of the mess you are in. Most of us do everything we can to avoid and ignore negative feelings and hope that they will disappear or resolve themselves. Unfortunately, this will never happen! Let's take a look at some of the most common negative emotions and how we can channel them in the right direction.

How to Use Anger and Rage to Your Advantage

Many of us find it difficult to deal with feelings of anger and rage, and when we dig a little deeper, we will find that this is because of how we were raised as children. Some of us were taught from a young age that getting angry is not a nice thing to do and that we should control our feelings of anger because they could lead us to do something we will end up regretting. As a result, we stuff our feelings of anger deep down inside ourselves, even if these feelings are justified, and we end up walking around with a chip on our shoulder. The other extreme of this is that some people are taught to use anger as a way to manipulate people into getting them to do what they want. People who live like this are always involved in screaming matches. There is nothing healthy about any of these approaches.

When you think about it, anger makes you feel alive, and so you can use that physical charge that it gives you to channel more energy into your gym routine. You can also use it as a powerful motivator to push you toward your long-term goals. For example, you might feel anger toward your sister for making fun of your weight; instead of lashing out and getting upset about these comments, use your rage as the foundation for positive change. And no, you are not basing your life decisions on the words and actions of others, but what you are doing is using them to your advantage when they are sent in your direction. A desire to prove to the people who mocked and taunted you when you were younger that you are capable of doing something worthwhile and making a positive impact on the world will provide the necessary fuel to propel you forward.

HOW TO USE ENVY TO YOUR ADVANTAGE

Envy is another emotion you can use to your advantage. Think about it, what do most people do when they experience feelings of jealousy? They waste their time and energy tearing the other person down. When you are envious, it is an indication that another person has something you desire. If you are envious of your friend's material possessions, start working at generating more money so you can experience the financial freedom required to buy what you want. If you feel jealous about the weight someone has lost while you sit in front of the TV every night stuffing your face with pizza, it's time to start making a serious weight loss plan. When you experience jealousy, evaluate your feelings and write out what you want and start working toward achieving those goals.

HOW TO USE ANXIETY TO YOUR ADVANTAGE

Do you ever feel anxious? It's a terrible feeling, right? The good news is that your bad habit of worrying can actually work in your favor if you allow it to. Fear can paralyze you, but when it is used in the right way, it can be one of the most powerful catalysts for success. There are two ways that this can work: first, it is a satisfying feeling to conquer your fears, so just think about how awesome you will feel once you've achieved something that you were afraid of—it's a great way to stay motivated. Second, you can use fear as the foundation required to start taking constructive action. For example, let's say your job is at risk because the company you are employed by is experiencing financial difficulty. This is a scary prospect; naturally, you are going to start thinking about how you are going to survive, how you are going to pay your bills and put food on the table. Most people will waste their time focusing on the worst-case scenario. They will spend so much energy thinking about all the bad things that could happen, that when they do finally lose their job, they are forced to take action. However, when you use your fear and anxiety as a tool to push you in the right direction, even if the worst does happen and you do end up losing your job, it won't affect you because you have prepared for the worst. It is impossible to get rid of fear, but you can manage it so you might as well take advantage of the emotion when it shows up.

If you are overwhelmed with feelings of anxiety, sit down and take some deep breaths to gain your composure. Get a pen and paper, draw a line down the middle of the paper and at the top of the paper write, "The things I'm afraid of on one side," and "The worst that could happen" on the other side—now start writing. Put that piece of paper to one side, get another sheet of paper and begin to brainstorm how you can make the most out of a bad situation. For example, your dream might be to quit your job, travel the world, and rent out your house. Now you've identified what you are afraid of and the worst-case scenario if it were to happen. For example, your fear might be that you get terrible tenants, not only do they fail to pay the rent, but they also ruin your house. The next step is to think about how you could solve this problem if it were to happen. Using the above example, your plan might be to make sure you've got enough money in the bank to cover the rent if they fail to pay, apply for the necessary insurance that will cover you for damages, and make arrangements to have your home redecorated as quickly as possible so you can get another tenant in. As well as taking the necessary financial precautions, you can also ask family and friends to recommend a tenant, so you feel confident that the person is less likely to wreck your home. This exercise proves that fear can be the spark required to trigger problem-solving and creative thinking.

The assumption is that fear means we are moving in the wrong direction—this is not the aim of fear. If you are afraid to make changes in your life, it is a positive sign! Why? Because it means you are stepping out of your comfort zone, which is one of the main requirements for success and progress. Consider the times in your life when you've had to push yourself to accomplish a major challenge. You probably felt an overwhelming sense of fear because you were doing something that wasn't familiar to you. But whatever the challenge was, you got there in the end, right? Never give fear the power to hold you back, and at the same time, don't go into battle with it. Accept fear as a natural human emotion and then work at moving toward your goal one step at a time. Everyone goes through life experiencing fear, but the difference between those who overcome it and those who don't is the ability to use your fears to your advantage instead of allowing them to paralyze you.

USING SADNESS AND DESPAIR TO YOUR ADVANTAGE

Sadness and despair are much more difficult to use as fuel to power you into the direction of success. However, it isn't impossible, and by using your imagination, you can use these emotions to your advantage. Let's say, you have just gone through a messy divorce and your best friend has decided to turn her back on you, which has all transpired within a few months. Unless events of this nature are handled in the right way, they can become a terrible distraction that will completely steal your focus.

The first step in coming to terms with such issues is to understand that your situation isn't going to last forever—the pain you are experiencing right now will subside over time. When we lose people we care about, it often opens the door to a period of deep self-reflection. Although these people are still alive, they played an important role in our lives and now they are gone. You are going to go through a grieving process in which you will mourn the loss of your loved ones. During this time, you will also begin to start putting things into perspective—things that were once of great importance to you will suddenly appear trivial in comparison to what has just happened. When you gain this type of clarity, you will experience a massive improvement in the area of time management and focus because you will realize that life is too short, and following your dreams and achieving your goals are the most important things to you. Now instead of spending all your time gossiping and watching TV, you will put your time to productive use and channel your energy into something worthwhile. At this point, self-discipline will get easier because you will get into the habit of focusing on the things that are going to help you achieve your goals.

There are some people who achieve a lifelong goal or dream in memory of a loved one. Some people find the inspiration to do extraordinary things at the worst moments in their lives. Losing a partner or family member to illness or a tragic accident can prompt this type of reaction in someone. A common example is someone who typically spends their life in front of the TV suddenly turning into a health and fitness fanatic so they can run a marathon to help raise money for a charity focused on raising money to fight the cancer that took the life of a friend or a loved one. Although they had no athletic ability whatsoever, doing something to raise positive awareness to prevent this type of tragedy taking place for others causes people to put their priorities in order.

If you've got creative goals, for example, you want to become a better artist or write a novel, you'll be encouraged to know that research suggests that negative circumstances can be a powerful driving force to get you to your final destination. A study conducted by Ghent University monitored the emotions and daily habits of 102 full-time creative professionals. The researchers found that participants were most productive on the days when they were not in the best of moods. Therefore, the evidence suggests that negative energy can be transformed into creative output. If you are the creative type, the next time you feel sad, angry, or distressed, immerse yourself in writing, music, art, or something of a similar nature.

HOW TO USE SHAME TO YOUR ADVANTAGE

Shame is another negative emotion that holds us back from going after what we want and engaging with the world. It is also important to mention here that shame and guilt are not the same—guilt is normal and healthy. When you have done something to offend someone or your actions are not lining up with your moral compass, you will feel guilty, and this feeling of guilt will lead you to apologize or rectify the situation. Shame, on the other hand, causes a person to feel that they are unworthy, and this is usually because of something they have experienced. A person who feels shame will keep telling themselves they are a bad person, or that they deserve what happened to them. It is difficult to put in the work required to move forward when your self-esteem has been destroyed. When you feel that you are fundamentally flawed, you will feel that you deserve the life you are currently living and that you don't deserve anything better. However, if you are determined to overcome feelings of shame, it's most definitely possible.

Brene Brown, author of *Daring Greatly*, provides us with a step-by-step account of how we can let go of shame in order to live a more productive and successful life. The first step is to confide in someone you can trust about your feelings. The aim here is to find acceptance from another person to make it easier to forgive yourself. If you don't feel comfortable opening up to someone you know, seek professional help from a counselor. Brown goes on to explain that when we let go of shame, we grow in compassion for ourselves and those around us. Once we can accept that everyone is human and we all make mistakes, you will start to believe that everyone deserves a second chance to make things right. Overcoming shame is an important step if you want to de-clutter your mind in order to focus on becoming all you were created to be.

It is natural to get discouraged when you put a lot of time and energy into a project and it doesn't work out. The good news is that if you look at it from the right angle, time is never wasted if you are doing something productive. In the next chapter, you will learn about two important principles that will encourage you to never give up.

CHAPTER 16:

THE PARETO PRINCIPLE AND STURGEON'S LAW

Most of us have experienced that discouraging feeling when we have put in hours of work, but the project doesn't turn out the way we had hoped. In this chapter, you will learn why it's normal to devote so much time to your work but still feel as if you haven't gotten anywhere with it. Additionally, you will learn why accepting this truth will motivate you to develop an even greater level of self-discipline. To achieve this motivation, we will study two approaches—The Pareto Principle and Sturgeon's Law.

STURGEON'S LAW

Theodore Sturgeon was a science fiction author, and in 1958 he wrote an article for *Venture* magazine. He had become frustrated at the way critics had labeled the science fiction genre as low quality. He argued that even though there was probably some truth in a lot of science fiction work being a low-quality genre, it's possible to say the same thing about everything else. His statement became known as Sturgeon's Law. In recent years, philosopher Daniel Dennett stated that Sturgeon's Law was one of the seven key tools for critical thinking, which is evidence that it is still relevant for writers and academics today.

THE PARETO PRINCIPLE

The Pareto principle is similar. In 1896, Vilfredo Pareto, an Italian economist published a paper highlighting the fact that eighty percent of the land in Italy was owned by twenty percent of the country's people. He came to this conclusion by observing that twenty percent of the pea plants in his garden produced eighty percent of the best pea pods. This observation was later termed "The law of the vital few" or the 80/20 rule. The Pareto Principle has become the rule of thumb and the basis for many business guidelines, the most common one being that eighty percent of your business comes from twenty percent of your customers.

HOW DO THESE LAWS APPLY TO ME?

With your understanding of Sturgeon's law, you are probably wondering why you should bother putting time and energy into a project if there is such a high chance of it being rubbish. The Pareto Principle is also off-putting because it tells us that our best results will come from only twenty percent of our work—so again, what's the point in trying? When evaluated in the right way, there are several important lessons about developing self-discipline you can take from these principles. First, they encourage us to accept that it's the norm to work hard without having an assurance of what's going to yield the highest results and what won't. For example, you might be a fiction author who has written a series of books over the course of two years. You put a tremendous amount of effort into each one of them, but three of them hardly sell, whereas one of the books becomes a smash hit and you become an award-winning author. If you had no understanding of the Pareto Principle, you might be disappointed that all of your others books have failed to achieve the same level of success, and it might discourage you from continuing on your writing journey. On the other hand, with knowledge of the Pareto Principle, you are motivated and encouraged to keep writing because you know that success will be inevitable with at least one of your books. Spurgeon's Law and the Pareto Principle help you keep a broader perspective, which is essential for maintaining your self-discipline and momentum as you work toward your goals.

Once you accept the reality that only a small percentage of your work will make a difference, it will give you the push you need not only to work harder but to work smarter. Successful CEOs understand this principle, which is why they are willing to take risks with new products and services and refuse to give up even though everything else has failed. They know that it's impossible for people to be successful all the time, and the easiest way to protect yourself against disappointment is to anticipate complications along the way.

When you look at it from the right perspective, the 80/20 rule is exciting. Even though eighty percent of your work won't get you the results you want, twenty percent of your work will provide you with everything you need. There is always going to be a degree of uncertainty because you don't know which projects will succeed and which ones will fail. It is normal to want to predict the future, but how boring would that be if you knew for certain that everything you were doing was going to be a success? To some extent, the majority of us thrive on uncertainty; and if you persevere, your very best work might be just around the corner. If you give up now, you will never know what the outcome of your hard work could have been. Top performers fail all the time, but they understand that all they need is a couple of major successes to set them up for life—the same principle applies to you too. It doesn't matter if you come up with some terrible ideas, what matters is that you keep going.

HOW TO HANDLE FAILURE

There is a lesson to learn from every failure; therefore, use your losses as a springboard to greater things. When something doesn't work out the way you had planned, evaluate it to find out what went wrong, and don't get hung up on the fact that it didn't work out. If you can't get anything out of it, at least it gave you the opportunity to practice self-discipline. When you discover what does work, build on it for repeated success. This might sound like common sense, but people struggle with this because there is such a huge difference between what worked and what they were expecting to work. Evaluating this takes self-discipline because when you have an emotional investment in something, it's difficult to put it to one side. What ends up happening is that because we are emotionally attached to something, we keep working at it even if it's burning a hole in our pocket, and being overly driven by a passion can have a negative effect on our psychological well-being. When this is looked at objectively, it's hard to understand. The person with no emotional attachment can look at the project and see that it's not working, as well as see *why* it's not working. But the person who has an emotional attachment to it will find it hard to admit they've made a mistake and pride will not allow them to walk away from a failing project.

On the other hand, if you are able to accept that your efforts are not going to give you the results you are looking for, you will develop the skill of knowing when to give up gracefully and start working on something else. Essentially, what you are doing is using wisdom to determine when it's time to sacrifice a fantasy and build on what's working for you.

When you train yourself to focus on what's happening in the present as opposed to the things that could have been and might have been in the past, you will ultimately become a lot more productive. Being self-disciplined and determined is important if you are going to achieve your goals; however, what you don't want to happen is that you become so engrossed in what you are doing that you exhaust yourself. In the next chapter, I will discuss how you can avoid this pitfall.

CHAPTER 17:

HOW TO AVOID BURNOUT

So far, you've spent sixteen chapters reading about how to build self-discipline and remain focused when you encounter circumstances and obstacles that deplete your willpower. But it is also important to understand that when you push yourself too far, you can do yourself some serious damage. In this chapter, I am going to talk about burnout and how you can avoid it. You will learn about the symptoms, how to recover, and why some people end up physically and emotionally destroyed because of the immense amount of pressure they place on themselves. Although it is possible to bounce back from stress and burnout, prevention is better than cure.

WHAT IS BURNOUT?

Stress is a normal part of life. Whether you experience it daily, weekly, or once a year, you will experience it at some point. When your circumstances become overwhelming, it becomes difficult to think straight or do anything productive. The inability to function due to stress is referred to as "brain freeze," and it typically lasts for a few minutes or sometimes a few hours. Stepping back from the problem or taking a break from work is usually all we need to get us back on track. It decreases anxiety levels and helps us regain self-control. However, when a person has completely burnt out, recovery is extremely difficult because he/she is no longer able to cope either mentally or physically with the demands of life. Burnout can reach a level where the person requires psychiatric assistance.

Burnout is a physical and mental state that causes low mood, exhaustion, the inability to make decisions, and hopelessness. Anyone can suffer burnout, whether you are a CEO of a large corporation, a single mother, or a part-time employee. It all depends on how much pressure you place on yourself, your personality, and your coping skills. People who suffer from burnout will often blame themselves for their inability to cope. They will compare themselves to their peers, experiencing the same conditions as they are, who are coping fine, and then jump to the conclusion that there is something fundamentally wrong with them. High achievers often suffer from burnout because they thrive off of demanding roles and will push themselves to the limit without taking the time out to rest and relax. This works for the short term, but it isn't a viable strategy over the long term. For example, if you are at the final stages of closing a large business deal, you will probably need to put in a few late nights to make sure that everything is in order. However, this only becomes a problem when work-life imbalance becomes the norm. As you are improving your self-discipline, it is important that you take the necessary precautions not to stretch yourself too far.

The good news about burnout is that it doesn't just creep up on you. Nobody feels fine one day and then burnt out the next. Therefore, as long as you pay attention to how you are feeling, you can prevent it. As strange as this may sound, it's important that you put a cap on your self-discipline. You can achieve this by learning how to say "no" to projects and tasks that leave you drained and stick to a healthy routine at the same time. It is imperative that you get at least seven hours of sleep per night, drink plenty of water throughout the day, and eat a balanced diet. This might sound like too much effort or that you are wasting time on things that are not going to help you reach your end goal. However, it is important to remember that if you don't take the time out to keep yourself healthy, you won't have the mental capacity to perform at a high level and make wise decisions. Remember, when you are tired, your will power is depleted; therefore, getting enough sleep and eating nutritious meals that will provide you with a good source of energy will increase your chances of success.

TAKE THE TIME OUT TO RELAX

If you overwhelm yourself with difficult decisions and endless tasks, it is inevitable that you will reach burnout. There is more to taking time out to relax than just enjoying yourself—it will allow you to recharge your batteries so you can perform at the highest level. Even members of the Special Forces and Shaolin monks aren't expected to work or train seven days a week. They understand that too much physical and mental pressure can have a negative effect on their ability to exercise self-control.

When you take time out to relax, make sure you do so properly, which means letting go of all thoughts about work. Don't keep checking your phone to see if a client has responded to any of your messages. Relaxation is about giving yourself a break from the stress and pressures of the outside world.

In general, it isn't the workload that drives people to burnout, it's the thought process that accompanies the workload. Everything boils down to choice and how you choose to view your experiences. If you don't enjoy your work and see it as a burden, eventually, you will start feeling the pressure. Alternatively, you can adopt the attitude that, although the task you are working on is demanding and will require that you put a lot of effort into it, in the long run, you will reap the benefits. It is also important to apply self-discipline to your workload, which will help reduce stress levels and highlight any potential problems before they start. Avoid trivial distractions and procrastination or your workload will pile up. Backlogs will force you to do an excessive amount of work in a short time frame, which can cause burnout—this is a form of self-induced stress and you can avoid it by being proactive.

Most people are motivated and excited at the start of a project, which is good, but you should also bear in mind that things might not always work out as planned, which is why you need a framework to work from.

THE IMPORTANCE OF SCHEDULING

At the beginning of any project, take time out to work out a schedule. In this way, you can come up with a realistic estimate of how much time you will need to put into the project. If you are not sure, ask someone who has more knowledge or experience than you do for advice. If you are still uncertain, assume that the project will take approximately one and a half times longer than you had expected. If you finish early, you can take the extra time you have available to relax or get a head start on the next project. If you do need the extra time, you haven't lost out on anything because you anticipated it from the beginning.

Personally, I find scheduling helpful when it comes to putting presentations together and writing up reports. Over time I have found that keeping spreadsheets of tasks and documenting the time it takes to complete each one has been very helpful, especially when it comes to my weekly planning. Although scheduling seems like a common-sense strategy for handling your workload, you would be surprised at how very few people implement this approach. One of the main reasons for not doing so is fear. Scheduling requires you to look closely at a project and it highlights the fact that there is going to be a lot of work involved. There are also going to be challenges, and you've got to take into consideration the fact that things might not work out the way you had originally planned. The only way to get around this is to acknowledge your fears and take action regardless. There will never come a time when you will wake up and feel confident about a difficult assignment. In fact, until you start working on the project, your anxiety levels will increase. The earlier you get into the habit of doing this, the less stressed you will become in the long run.

WHAT IF I'VE ALREADY REACHED BURNOUT?

I can hear you saying, *"Okay, these tips you've provided are great but I'm already exhausted and the thought of another day of work makes me physically sick."* The only way to recover from burnout is to take some time off to give your body and mind a break. If you had broken your arm or were suffering from bronchitis, you would need to take time off to recover. The same applies to burnout. You might need one week or two of rest. Just make sure you go back to work when you are fully recovered, not when you think you have to. If you are employed, let your employer know; if you are self-employed, let your clients know. Fortunately, work-life balance is important to employers, so in most cases, you will get the sympathy and understanding that you deserve.

During the recovery process, spend time reflecting on what you can learn from the experience. Remember, experiencing burnout doesn't mean that you can't cope with your job or you are a failure. However, it is a clear indication that you need to change the way you approach your work. When you are willing to evaluate what has gone wrong and what you could have done differently, it will provide a strong foundation for you to make constructive changes. Think back to the time when you began to show signs of burnout and write out a list of the strategies you could implement to prevent it from happening again. For example, was your burnout triggered when your work colleague went on vacation and you agreed to take over his workload? This would have been the perfect opportunity to use the power of "No," and inform your colleague that you've got too much to do already and won't be able to take on any more projects.

Striking the right balance between safeguarding your mental health and pushing yourself to the limit is a skill, and it will take a while before you perfect it.

CONCLUSION

Congratulations, you have read the entire book! You are not average, neither are you ordinary, you are an extraordinary person! How can I say this with such confidence? Because you have achieved something that most people never accomplish—you have read a book from start to finish. You have taken the initiative to learn about the habits required to improve your level of self-discipline. If you felt that you didn't have any discipline before you started reading this book, you can celebrate the fact that there has been a definite improvement because it takes persistence, determination, and discipline to see something through to the end.

You might be thinking, *"Well, I only read a book,"* but I would like to remind you that it's one positive step in the right direction. Remember, willpower is like a muscle, and the more you use it, the stronger it will become. You are not going to develop the discipline of Bill Gates overnight—it's going to take some time, but you've got to start somewhere.

Now that you've read the book, it's time to take action, take some time out, reassess your life, and decide how you're going to start this journey. Don't make life difficult and give yourself an unrealistic target. Start with adopting one habit for five minutes each day or waking up half an hour earlier than you are used to. Your life is a reflection of the decisions you have made, and if you want a better future, it's essential that you start making better decisions. It is possible for you to have the life you desire, but it starts with taking responsibility for the state of your life at this present moment. Whether it's your finances, lifestyle, relationships, or your mindset, it is up to you to make the required changes to improve. The following quote fully embodies the point I am making:

> *"You must take personal responsibility. You cannot change the circumstances, the seasons or the wind, but you can change yourself."* ~ *Jim Rohn*

Self-discipline is a lifestyle. It's not something you put to use when you want to achieve a goal. Self-discipline should be embedded in your character. We look at the rich and famous and envy their lives, but it took many years of making private sacrifices to get where they are today. Your character behind closed doors is more important than the character that people see in public. Author, speaker, and pastor John Maxwell held a lecture at a university, and one of the students asked the following question: *"John, your leadership principles sound life changing, the problem is that I don't know anyone who will allow me to lead them. What can I do about this?"* Maxwell responded, *"This is a very good question. You can start by leading yourself."* Before you can help anyone, you must first help yourself.

You picked up this book with the knowledge that you were in the wrong place and needed help—it might not feel that way, but you are in a good place. If you feel that your goals are unattainable, you are in a good place, because that's how every successful person felt at the beginning of their journey. What they wanted to achieve looked impossible, but they took action every day to get where they are now. As you continue repeating good habits, they will become like second nature and you will start operating optimally on autopilot. *yes*

Self-discipline is the key to success. You might have all the knowledge, talent, or skill in the world, but because of a lack of discipline, you will never make it. I believe there are better basketball players than Michael Jordan, better singers than the late Whitney Houston, and people with better business ideas than Elon Musk, but the world will never know them because they have no self-discipline.

Finally, I would like to remind you that there is a lot more to your self-discipline journey than you think. Whatever you want to achieve in life is going to have an impact on others, and if you fail to arrive at your place of purpose, the people who you would have had an effect on will never know that it's possible to achieve *their* dreams.

One of the reasons why I write books is because I read many books by people who motivated me to get where I am today. I went to seminars and listened to motivational speakers to equip me with the knowledge I needed to get to my next level. If the people who gave me access to the information I required to achieve my dreams had given up because of a lack of discipline, there is a possibility that I wouldn't be where I am today, which means I wouldn't be writing this book and providing you with the knowledge you need to improve your self-discipline in order to succeed.

You will never know what you are capable of until you start taking action and doing proactive, constructive things. Don't waste another second—apply the principles you have learned and expect a radical transformation in your life.

I wish you every success on your journey to mastering self-discipline!

THANKS FOR READING!

I really hope you enjoyed this book and, most of all, got more value from it than you had to give.

It would mean a lot to me if you left an Amazon review—I will reply to all questions asked!

Simply find this book on Amazon, scroll to the reviews section, and click "Write a customer review".

Or alternatively please visit www.pristinepublish.com/disciplinereview to leave a review.

Be sure to check out my email list, where I am constantly adding tons of value. The best way to get on the list currently is by visiting www.pristinepublish.com/morningbonus and entering your email.

Here I'll provide actionable information that aims to improve your enjoyment of life. I'll update you on my latest books, and I'll even send free e-books that I think you'll find useful.

Kindest regards,

Daniel Walter

REFERENCES

Brownell, K., (2021). Kelly D. Brownell's research works | Yale University, CT (YU). ResearchGate.

Clear, J. (2021). *Atomic Habits.* Random House.

Goggins, D. (2018). *Can't Hurt Me: Master Your Mind and Defy the Odds.* USA: Lioncrest Publishing.

King, A. (2019). *SELF DISCIPLINE FOR SUCCESS: How to use the power of Self Discipline to get the life you want. Simple Strategies to change your mindset and improve your willpower to achieve your goals.* USA: Independently published.

Luciani, J., 2015. *Why 80 Percent of New Year's Resolutions Fail.* U.S. News.

Moore, R. (2019). *I'm Worth More: Realize your real value and earn your success.* New York, United States: Quercus.

Moore, R. (2019b). *Start Now, Get Perfect Later* (Reprint). New York, United States: Teach Yourself.

Ray, G. (2018). *Self Discipline: A How-To Guide to Stop Procrastination and Achieve Your Goals in 10 Steps Including 10*

Day Bonus Online Coaching Course to Master Self-Discipline and Build Daily Goal-Crushing Habits. USA: Amazon Digital Services LLC – Kdp Print Us.

Roll, R. (2013). *Finding Ultra: Rejecting Middle Age, Becoming One of the World's Fittest Men, and Discovering Myself.* New York, United States: Three Rivers Press.

Tolle, E. (2001). *The Power of Now: A Guide to Spiritual Enlightenment.* London, England: Hodder and Stoughton.

Willink, J., & Babin, L. (2017). *Extreme Ownership: How U.S. Navy SEALs Lead and Win (New Edition).* New York, United States: St. Martin's Publishing Group.

Willink, J., & Babin, L. (2018). *The Dichotomy of Leadership: Balancing the Challenges of Extreme Ownership to Lead and Win* (1st ed.). New York, United States: St. Martin's Press.

Made in the USA
Columbia, SC
29 November 2023

deed6604-27d0-4638-93af-a93c89680407R01